Don Pinn

African
JOURNEYS

GW00394092

Don Pinnock

African
JOURNEYS

DOUBLE
STOREY
a juta company

in association with Getaway magazine

First published 2003
by Double Storey Books,
a division of Juta & Co. Ltd,
Mercury Crescent, Wetton, Cape Town
in association with *Getaway* magazine

ISBN 1-919930-40-X

© 2003 Don Pinnock

All rights reserved

Permission to reproduce any of these essays in a magazine rests with *Getaway*, to whom application should be made

Design and layout by Jenny Young
Printing by Creda Communications,
Epping, Cape Town

Contents

Preface

Travelling in Africa has its dangers, but they are not always what you would expect.

There are the lesser – almost insignificant – dangers such as when a large male lion locks its golden eyes on yours as you step out from behind a bush for a better photograph and you realise you may have just entered his food chain. Or, as a battle-scarred hippo begins a jaw-snapping charge, you realise you're standing between him and his favourite pool.

These are mere fleas on the hide of a far greater danger: entrancement. The list of those who succumbed reads like a Who's Who of travel: Livingstone, Speke, Burton, Stanley, Ibn Batuta, Napoleon, Baker, Roosevelt, Thoreau and many more, all sucked into the Dark Continent like wayward ants into a vacuum cleaner.

To travel this strange, ancient continent can be like stepping back in time and having cherished romantic blinkers ripped from your face. It has the greatest diversity of creatures, the most bewildering gene pool, some of the remotest unexplored areas, disease and the world's worst poverty. It also has the sweetest, most hospitable people I've ever met.

It is – and I use the word with the weight it deserves – interesting. The danger of entrancement, of course, is that in luring you in, it changes you utterly. If it cannot, it will surely drive you mad.

Each month, as a writer and photographer for *Getaway* magazine, I set off to some place I expect 600 000 readers will enjoy. With some surprise, on compiling the stories for this book, I realised I'd been doing it for seven years. How time slides.

I've had magnificent adventures: following in the footsteps of David Livingstone, being part of a non-stop trip from Cape to Cairo, traversing the entire Okavango Delta in a dugout canoe, searching for rock art in the central Sahara. *Getaway* journalists set themselves some crazy challenges, then see if they can meet them. As a lifestyle it's compelling, and I have come to understand Livingstone's crazy compulsion to experience ever new and intriguing places.

Good friends who, sadly, spend much of their lives in traffic jams, in offices and at computers, now seldom ask me where I've been. If I happen to tell them, they generally groan, then talk about the wrong job they're in. So I usually say something vague like 'Oh, just another trip'.

In these seven years I have been utterly, happily changed by Africa. I am more tolerant of difference, less concerned about comfort, stare at stars more often, spend blissful hours watching creatures like suricates at play, empathise with trees, enjoy the taste of jackalberries and get toweringly angry with people, corporations and governments who despoil land for profit.

Personal change is painless if you don't resist. I can recommend it.

This book has been made possible because of my extraordinary good fortune of working with a team of people who are comfortably eccentric and have a passion for travel, photography and the weaving of words. It also helps to have a polymath editor like David Bristow, who seems to know almost every place, creature and geological formation in Africa.

'If you have a good idea, then go check it out' has been a comment preceding many of the stories in this book. Those who might express misgivings about some odd adventure David will inevitably fix with a steely glare and remind them that he is the editor, so they'd just better get out and try. It seems the way to run a successful travel magazine.

I am, of course, often away from home, out of contact and in doubtful circumstances, things my family deal with devoid of complaint and with boundless support. Thanks, guys. The fun we have on the occasions you travel with me is, I hope, some measure of reward.

Don Pinnock

Cape Town, 2003

A missionary road to the interior

Likeability is not a characteristic normally associated with explorers. Burton, although undoubtedly brilliant, was considered haughty and obnoxious. Captain Cook flogged sailors and cut the ears off thieving Polynesians. Stanley was bumptious. Cortez killed and pillaged. Out beyond the boundaries of their civilisation, it seems, Europeans had to be steely and singularly bloody-minded.

So I didn't expect to like David Livingstone. Behind the screen of public adulation, he was a man of questionable character. He spent only six years with his subjugated wife, Mary, left her in absolute poverty while he travelled, and failed miserably as a father.

Yet Livingstone was to become the hero of England and the darling of Queen Victoria. As a child labourer in the cotton mills of Blantyre, Scotland, the tenacious Scot had studied Latin by propping a book on the spinning jenny. He was seen as a man of simple, honest origins who had made good. But he considered himself a failure. And, in many respects, he was. Not only missionaries or traders followed his trails, but gunrunners and slavers as well. Many young missionaries who answered his call to open Africa to trade and Christianity died of malaria.

Livingstone sponged shamelessly off his father-in-law, the saintly Robert Moffat, badmouthed other missionaries, condemned Africans who couldn't abide by his narrow Christianity as backsliding fools and made life hell for Europeans travelling with him, fearing they would steal the glory of his discoveries. While he is characterised by some as everything a Christian should be – noble and spiritual with the common touch – there are others who consider him a mean-spirited clod. If psychotherapy had been available in the mid-19th century, he would have been a prime candidate.

But the man walked, by rough estimate, 42,000 kilometres through uncharted areas of a continent believed by Europe of the 19th century to contain monsters, cannibals or worse. He traversed pitiless deserts; followed great rivers still wild and unpredictable today; stood, amazed, beside shimmering lakes and waterfalls of the Great Rift Valley; documented, meticulously, the customs of unheard-of peoples and the strange flora and fauna of a then Dark Continent.

He charmed warlike tribes with a mirror and a magnifying glass and was adored by powerful chiefs as well as men he had snatched from the hands of Arab slavers. And he wrote ripping travel diaries.

When he died, his faithful attendants buried his heart and entrails beside a tree, dried his body like a *kapenta* fish, carried it through dangerous savanna for 1500 kilometres – then followed it to Britain.

More than a century after his death he remains mythical. The idea of setting off in a well-equipped 4x4 to see where he went – and to get a sense of how Africa had changed since he plodded through – was irresistible.

As my wife, Patricia, and I got beyond the borders of South Africa, however, the extraordinary respect for Livingstone shown by even simple peasants caused us to ask another question: just what did this man mean to Africa?

::

Drizzle from a grey winter sky followed us as we slipped out of Cape Town and over Du Toit's Kloof Pass. But it soon relented. By the time we were winding up Michell's Pass, bars of sunlight were picking out patches of bright fynbos.

Enticed by an old stone restaurant named Die Tolhuis in the mountain fastness, we stopped for an early lunch. It really had been a tollhouse: 3d a wheel, 2d a horse or ox and

a ha'penny for each pig, goat or sheep. In 1852 Livingstone, penniless after 11 years up north, would have driven his dishevelled wagon and equally dishevelled family past it on the way back to Cape Town. Had he paid the toll? His diaries do not mention it.

Ceres drifted by, neat and green, then we began our long haul across the dusty roads of the Great Karoo. Hottentotskloof, Sutherland, Fraserburg and a great, flat emptiness – we were already way off the tourist route.

It was Sunday, and Carnarvon, when we nosed into the dorp, seemed to have been evacuated. The hotel was closed, the restaurant was barred and a guesthouse dark. I banged on the hotel door, hoping someone could tell us where we could stay. After I'd given up and begun walking away, a man appeared.

'Hotel's closed,' he said, stating the obvious. Then he peered at the artwork on the door of our Mitsubishi Colt and asked: 'Who's David Livingstone?'

We drove round a bit, then found a deserted camp site, the grass dry and frostbitten. But it had hot water. The build-up to the trip and the bumpy driving had exhausted us. Dust had poured into the back, turning everything grimy brown. We flipped up the rooftop tent but couldn't find the portable neon light. We forgot where we'd packed the snacks – cooking supper seemed out of the question. Soon after sunset the temperature plunged to zero.

Patricia huddled in the torch-lit tent, cold and miserable. 'Why are we doing this?' she asked. I thought of our children at home (rather better provided for than Livingstone's) heating a pre-cooked, frozen meal and probably jostling for space with our Labrador round a roaring fire, and couldn't come up with an answer. All night the dogs of Carnarvon barked at each other, and now and then a donkey brayed hideously. It was a miserable night.

Next morning we stuffed plastic bags in the canopy's leaky joints and nosed into town. There we found the Ou Kraal Kombuis. It had once been the Adelphi Café and Cinema and is now a shop, dance hall and restaurant, run by Barbara van den Berg. Versatile building. Breakfast was generous and cheap and we left town with a rising sun, feeling guardedly excited. Deep in Africa we would remember that camp site as one of the best. Our learning curve was just coming off the baseline.

On the endless-seeming flat road between Carnarvon and Prieska we met Avi Morris, a *karretjiemens* with a tatty wagon, two ragged donkeys and a young foal, which was tied up in a bag next to him. He said he was a woodcutter. 'There's no wood around here, just scrub bush,' I commented.

'Yes,' he sighed, 'that's why I'm going to Prieska.'

He had been on the road, all alone with his three asses, for two days. It would take another three, we estimated, for him to reach Prieska. He had no money and the road stretched away from him like an arrow. Time past, time future: Avi Morris and the great blue sky, still plying the old missionary road to the north in a creaking wagon.

'Wagon-travelling in Africa is a prolonged system of picnicking,' Livingstone had written. 'Excellent for the health and agreeable to those who are not over fastidious about trifles, and who delight in the open air.' Looking doubtfully at the old man and the bleak, winter-crisped Karoo, we wondered about that.

The Mary Moffat Museum in Griekwastad is an interesting place, with pictures of the sad-eyed Victorian lady, and a fine old pulpit. There was also an old photograph of her grave, somewhere on the Lower Zambezi floodplain, but no caption to tell us exactly where. We pushed on further, overnighting at the moody and delightful Witsand Nature Reserve with its generous cottages and strange, growling dunes.

We arrived in Kuruman three days after leaving the Cape – it had taken Livingstone two months. In Britain, when the young Livingstone was looking for a cause, Robert Moffat had lured him to Kuruman. There was a vast plain to the north, he told the eager young man, over which the sun rose on 'the smoke of a thousand villages where no missionary has ever been'.

When the weary oxen pulled Livingstone's wagon into Kuruman in July 1841, it was the northernmost Christian mission in Africa, built near the eye of an eternal spring. As it was then, the Moffat Mission is today a place of peace and tranquillity, a truly spiritual centre where we spent two happy days researching in the mission's excellent library and holding hands in the Memorial Garden. Its gentle director, Richard Aitken, and his wife, Jane, made us welcome, in the old missionary tradition.

Holy ground, it seemed to me as I listened to the morning prayers in the church Moffat built, is a simple thing. It's a place where generations have laboured at soul work. It creates harmony: simple as that.

Kuruman was the most important outpost of the London Missionary Society, but the young Livingstone was soon disillusioned with the place. He chafed to head north. With another missionary, Edwards, and his wife, he got his way, and together they established a mission station at Mabotsa, near present-day Zeerust, in 1843.

There Livingstone nearly lost his life. He was encouraged by the local people to shoot a troublesome lion, but he merely wounded it and it leapt at him, shaking him 'like a terrier dog does a rat' and fracturing his right arm. He felt, he said, a sort of dreaminess in which there was no sense of pain. His assistant shot the lion and saved his life. His arm, however, set badly and was ever after weakened.

Back at Kuruman, Moffat's eldest daughter, Mary, nursed him back to health. Under an almond tree in the Kuruman garden the young David went down on one knee and proposed marriage to her. She was, he wrote to friends, 'a matter-of-fact lady, a little thick black-haired girl, sturdy and all I want'. Still today there are debates about whether the union was based on love or the expectation, current at the time, that every missionary needed a wife to look after him.

Under giant syringa trees, sprinkling yellow winter leaves over the mission, there is today a broad wooden arrow pointing north with the words 'Missionary Road to the Interior'. Livingstone had named the way north God's Highway. We took the sign as our cue and hit the missionary's trail once more, a little sad to leave the peaceful mission.

By a remarkable set of coincidences we made contact with a resident in the Zeerust area, Arto Toivonen, who had located the mission site of Mabotsa. It's on the edge of a village named Gopane, and was on no modern map we could find and in no guidebook. It was there that the missionary first met his only convert, Chief Sechele of the Bakwena. All that's left now is foundation stones quarried by Livingstone and a sign under a tree marking it as his first mission: 1843–1846. There the rains failed, the Bakwena moved on and Livingstone returned to Kuruman.

In Zeerust, where we went for diesel, was another sign pointing north and an indication of the AIDS crisis we would encounter throughout our trip: 'Monty's Tombstones. Deposit only R25. Lay-bys accepted.' Wherever we travelled, the undertakers were doing a stiff trade.

The Livingstones' honeymoon was a 12-day trip to their new home, not Mabotsa but a second station Livingstone had begun at Tshongwane. During the two difficult years they spent there, Livingstone indulged in his passion for exploration, travelling east to the Magaliesberg. But he had heard tales of a great lake to the north and began making plans – in defiance of the wishes of the London Missionary Society.

Drought forced the people, and the missionary couple, to move again and they settled on the Kolobeng River further west.

For us, crossing the border into Botswana was like moving from the Third World into the First. The place was prosperous, the people seemed well educated and polite and the main roads were in good condition. These were the descendants of the tribes among whom Livingstone laboured. Wise chiefs, good policies plus diamonds and cattle have transformed them into one of the wealthiest nations in Africa. We overnighted with friends in Gaborone – a modern, booming city – then set off west to search for Kolobeng, until then a small star in an atlas.

At this new site Livingstone built the only real home his family would enjoy with him. There he and the community erected a church and dug a canal to bring river water to the mission's croplands. The challenge exhilarated him. In a letter he criticised missionaries languishing 'down in the Colony'. They should be 'right up here, riding on the world's backbone and snuffing like zebras the free, pure, delightful air of the great western desert!'

UNDER THE MANGO TREE
WHICH THEN STOOD HERE
HENRY M STANLEY MET
DAVID LIVINGSTONE
10 NOVEMBER 1871

This Monument was erected by the Government of Tanganyika Territory and the bronze plate contributed by the Royal Geographical Society in 1927.

At Kolobeng Livingstone built, farmed, healed the sick and preached to Sechele's people. Mary taught in the school they'd built, cooked their meals and tended her children, Robert and Agnes (she was to bear six children, two of whom died in Africa, and a third, Robert, as a young soldier in the American Civil War). In 1841, against the wishes of the worried tribe, who feared the wrath of their ancestors, Livingstone baptised Sechele.

We rolled across the Kolobeng River and turned through a gate. After a while Alfred Piet came trotting up. He's warden to almost nothing: Livingstone's house is now just a ring of foundation stones, the church even less obvious. The most noticeable remnants are a stone seat upon which Livingstone's patients sat and a circle of stones marking the grave of the couple's fourth child, Elizabeth.

Childbearing would ruin Mary's health (she suffered a mild stroke with each of the last two) and curtail any sense of achievement in mission work. In Victorian tradition, she would have no choice in the matter.

Livingstone would later boast of his self-sufficiency at Kolobeng, but his letters to Moffat told a different story. Requests were endless: 'I may as well tell you some more of our wants,' he penned; 'a trowel; large and small beads; a ladle and bullet mould; heifers if you can get them at any price; she goats; a musket if you have one to spare; vine cuttings; fruit stones for seed; pictures; the large vice mentioned.'

Livingstone, who had banned Chief Sechele (also the tribe's chief rainmaker) from invoking rain (and from polygamy) as a price for salvation, was blamed for the droughts at Tshongwane and Kolobeng. Rain fell all round, people noticed, but not on the mission. His own children were half starved. Livingstone dealt with his growing problems in his typical manner: he planned an exploration trip.

Teaming up with a wealthy hunter, William Cotton Oswell, Livingstone set off across the trackless Kalahari in June 1849, to find the 'great lake' he had heard of. They passed through what are now Lephepe and Serowe, then northwest through the thirstlands to Letlhakane to the Botete River. They nearly died from lack of water and some oxen perished from being bitten by tsetse fly. On the first day of August they stood on the shores of Lake Ngami.

We took a more easterly route, overnighting at a comfortable camp site beside the Marang Hotel in Francistown, then travelling west through the Makgadikgadi Pans to Maun. After a laid-back evening of beers and travel chatter at Audi Camp and a well-earned sleep, we tracked down the Nhabe River to search for the fabled Lake Ngami. It had disappeared.

By GPS reckoning we were in the dead centre of the lake, but all that surrounded us was flat yellow grass with a watchful patrol of vultures overhead. Later enquiries established that it

had dried up 20 years before, victim of the curious cyclical tilting of the Okavango basin. We rolled out the canopy, broke out the table and chairs and sipped Earl Grey tea, thinking about the terrible hardships that had befallen the missionary there on his second trip to the lake.

When reports of the lake's discovery reached London, Livingstone was awarded a gold medal by the Royal Geographical Society. Oswell took a back seat.

A year after his first visit, however, Livingstone returned to Ngami, this time with Mary and two small children in tow. It took them four months and ten days. It was an awful journey.

'In some parts we had to travel both day and night continuously for want of water,' he diarised, 'and then tie up the oxen to prevent them running away 'till we had dug wells. I lost four in pitfalls made for game, two from drought, one by a lion....'

The two children went down with malaria first; soon all his men were sick. At that time no one suspected the mosquito as the vector for malaria, and one winces to read Livingstone's complaint that he 'could not touch a square half inch of the bodies of the children unbitten after a single night's exposure'. Using a mixture of jalap resin, calomel, rhubarb and quinine – a remedy hit on by trial and error, which was to become known as the Livingstone Pill – he cured them.

After her return to Kolobeng, Mary, weakened by fever, gave birth to Elizabeth and, in childbirth, had a stroke which was to leave her face temporarily paralysed. Two weeks later the child died. As she succumbed she gave a piercing cry, a sound, Livingstone wrote, which would haunt him to the end of eternity.

Almost a year later, in 1851, the family was back in a wagon heading north once again (to the horror of Livingstone's mother-in-law, Mary Moffat). This time they took a more easterly route across the dead-flat plains of Makgadikgadi. Like a recurrent nightmare, thirst again overtook them, this time in the terrible Mababe Depression.

Eventually, miraculously, they entered the territory of Chief Sebetwane of the Makololo tribe and, after some hacking, the Linyanti River. When they reached Sebetwane's capital, named after the river, the party was given a tumultuous welcome. Within weeks, however, the chief died from pneumonia. As luck goes, Livingstone seems to have been a veritable Jonah to the Africans he befriended.

After a few nights back at Audi Camp in Maun – gathering our strength to follow the spectre of Livingstone's wagons northwards – we teamed up with two solo travellers, German Roland Richter and South African Justin Brogan, and headed for Chobe National Park. Our goal was Kudumane Village, just south of the park entrance, where we hoped to spend the night. It was a mere 130 kilometres away. How deceptive distance can be off the main roads in Africa.

The road to Chobe was in reality a maze of tracks, none signposted and many just thick sand. We arrived at the gate of Moremi Wildlife Reserve in error, tracked back to a village named Shukumukwa and eventually hung onto the GPS for dear life, careering through wild places in fading light until we ended up, almost by accident, in Kudumane.

Being lost in the wilderness didn't feel good. For Livingstone it would have been far more testing: most of the time he had only the vaguest idea of where he was or what perils lay ahead. We felt a creeping respect for the man.

Kudumane is a Tsegu San village with mud-walled, thatched-roof huts, goats, donkeys and beautiful, petite, naked children everywhere. For ten pula each we were given a camp site, then we whiled away our time discussing Tsegu traditions and the San names of stars with the locals.

As the sky deepened to purple-black, the Milky Way sparkled to life from horizon to horizon. In the woodland a hyena whooped as we prepared for bed. As he took his leave, one of the San, Mandwar Sebinelo, turned and said, almost as an afterthought: 'Our gods will stay with you.' It felt strangely reassuring.

We rolled out of the village before the sun rose and headed up yet another frightful sandy track. If this was the main road to a large national park, they were catering for nothing but intrepid and well-equipped travellers.

Inside the park, though, the roads were better. We soon met wise-looking elephants, batty-eyed giraffes, skittish zebras and wildebeest, a tawny eagle on every next dead tree, lilac-breasted rollers, pale chanting goshawks and a lone kori bustard.

Despite the claim at the park offices in Maun that all camp sites in Chobe were full, we drove up to the Savuti Gate and were offered a fine site behind a bombproof blockhouse, which turned out to be the elephantproof ablution building. The reason for the structure's solidity soon became clear. As we sat round preparing lunch, a jumbo with serviceable tusks wandered up to investigate. We suddenly figured that inside the vehicles would be a good place to eat.

That evening, Justin nearly had a steak snatched from the tailgate of his vehicle by a huge spotted hyena and we were confined to the ablution building for a bit while an elephant patrolled the gate. Everyone retired to the safety of their rooftop tents except Justin – who had a ground tent. Patricia lay awake for quite a while worrying about him, expecting more customers for his alluring camp cooking.

Chobe is an extraordinarily wild-feeling place, with minimal roads (tracks, really), few people and vast areas of mopane woodland and combretum. At times you gaze across rippling grass to the horizon; in other places the trees restrict your view to a few metres. Elephants and tawny eagles ruled, raucously attended by yellow-billed, red-billed and grey hornbills. Every now and then a Swainson's francolin would sprint ahead of our 4x4, kicking up sand as it dived into the verge grass.

Travelling up the Savuti Channel, dead on Livingstone's trail, we found the plain broken by several hills with complicated San names such as Gobatsaa (leopard), Damagosera (kudu),

LIVINGSTONE'S JOURNEYS IN AFRICA

Qumxhwaa (cave) and some stark pans. Livingstone, too, would have marvelled at huge baobabs on the slopes and listened with satisfaction to the soft calls of green pigeons. Mere emptiness can be frightening, but wilderness is somehow comforting and confidential.

From Savuti we headed northwest towards Linyanti, Sebetwane's capital, but elephants had pushed trees over the track and deep sand had built up from floods. So we headed northwards instead, past the Gcoha Hills and through the Chobe Forest Reserve to Katchekabwe and the Chobe River.

When Sebetwane died, Livingstone and Oswell, who was again travelling with him, left Mary and the wagons and rode north to visit a river people, the Sesheke or Borotse. They were amazed to find a river which was nearly half a kilometre wide, with huge floodplains. They had found the Chobe, and Livingstone rightly concluded it to be a main feeder of the Zambezi. He now knew where that great African waterway was, and he began to dream.

When Livingstone returned from the Chobe, his missionary skin had split like a chrysalis and a full-blown explorer had emerged. Africa beckoned irresistibly. The man who had caught the world's attention with Lake Ngami now had to overcome his greatest obstacle – the burden of his family.

He wrote to the London Missionary Society that he needed three years' freedom from family responsibilities. Instead of leaving Mary and the children in Kuruman, he trekked with them to Cape Town. They presented a strange spectacle: people stared. After 11 years in trackless Africa, it was evident that the world had passed them by. Livingstone found he had even lost the knack of stairs and turned round to go down as if on a ladder.

With no doubt mixed feelings, Livingstone booked his family on a ship to England with virtually no plan for their support. He simply assumed the Missionary Society would care for them. As it turned out, this didn't happen. The LMS was unhappy with Livingstone's non-missionary adventures and felt little responsibility towards his uninvited family, who became paupers dependent on handouts from distant family and friends. Mary, under impossible stress and far from the Africa she understood, began drinking heavily.

It has been suggested by several biographers that Livingstone's main reason for exiling his family from Africa was that if Mary had remained anywhere on the continent, they would have lived together from time to time and more children would have been conceived. An explorer simply could not afford an endless procession of children. More probably, Mary didn't get on well with her fussy mother and couldn't bear the thought of Kuruman without David.

While in Cape Town, Livingstone had taken instruction in mapping and navigation from the Astronomer Royal, Thomas Maclear, who was soon confident that his pupil had the principles of sextant and compass sussed. The men talked about the possibility of a trip from the west coast of Africa to the east, clear across the continent, and the chance of finding the great lakes rumoured to be in the centre of Africa.

When Livingstone arrived back at Kolobeng, he found his house smashed and looted by Boers, who had accused him of gun running. This simply hardened his resolve to head north again. He was not without fears, however.

'Am I on the way to die in Sebetwane's country?' he wrote in his diary. 'Have I seen the last of my wife and children? My soul, whither wilt thou emigrate? Where wilt thou lodge the first night after leaving the body?'

In May 1853 Livingstone was back at Linyanti. Shortly afterwards, he was staring in wonder at the great moving waters of the Zambezi River. One of the greatest expeditions of the 19th century was about to begin.

We were acutely conscious of having abandoned our own family as we watched the sun fall over Buffalo Ridge Camp, where we overnighted above the Chobe floodplain. It was wild and we were rather lonely and far from home. Each time, before entering a new country, the feeling would return. We sat, tapping e-mail messages home, fretting over the absence of anything in the inbox. Had they forgotten about us?

At sunrise we headed through eastern Chobe to fill up with our last gulp of cheap Botswana diesel before joining the queue of long-haul trucks at the Kazungula Ferry across the flooding Zambezi. Moneychangers flapped wads of notes at us hopefully; one offered us diamonds 'cheap, cheap'.

Our destination was Zambia, and we were finally wedged ahead of a huge road hauler on the shuddering ferry deck. The precarious craft fought its way across the surging waters and deposited us safely into the hands of easy-going border officials on the far shore.

'Where are you going?' a smart-looking officer asked.

'We're in transit.'

'Where to?'

'Ujiji and Zanzibar.'

'Eh, eh, eh, big journey!' Stamp.

'Is that a picture of David Livingstone on your truck?'

'Yes, sure....'

'Good man, that one. Have a safe journey.'

We limped into the town of Livingstone over impossibly potholed tar, tired and hungry, and discovered the green lawns of Fawlty Towers Backpackers and the mixed delights of the Funky Monkey Restaurant.

That night we turned in, to the dull roar of Mosi-oa-Tunya, the smoke that thunders. Next day, we agreed, we'd visit the falls, replenish our supplies, then get ready to follow the brown, flooding Zambezi, the river which would fire, then utterly destroy, Livingstone's greatest African dream.

Down the wild river

The plan was insane. After months of dehydrating himself through the Kalahari Desert, David Livingstone planned to ride his plodding white ox named Sinbad from the Chobe River to Luanda – from the eastern tip of the Caprivi Strip to the Atlantic Ocean. Then he would walk right across to the Indian Ocean. Nobody he knew of had taken such a daring trip. He had no idea if rivers, lakes or hostile tribes blocked the way. Traders, he would write, had told him there were many English in Luanda. 'Thither I prepared to go,' he wrote, 'and the prospect of meeting with countrymen seemed to overbalance the toils of the longer march.' That was odd, considering that he spent most of his life in Africa avoiding his fellow countrymen.

The party – Livingstone and 27 Makololo porters – had three muskets, a rifle and a double-barrelled shotgun plus ten kilos of beads, a small tent, a sheepskin blanket, a horse rug, some tea, coffee and sugar, a sextant and some spare clothes 'to be used when we reached civilised life'.

'I had always found', he commented, 'that the art of successful travel consisted in taking as few impedimenta as possible.' One wonders, then, why he needed so many porters.

He left the Makololo town of Linyanti (now in Namibia) in November 1853, and arrived in Luanda a year later. He had suffered almost constantly from malaria – 27 attacks – and was reduced to 'almost a skeleton'.

Under the care of Luanda's bishop, and slightly recovered, Livingstone had been offered passage back to England by sea. He refused. 'I resolved to decline the tempting offers of my naval friends,' he penned in his diary, 'and take my Makololo companions to their chief [at Linyanti] with a view of trying to make a path from his country to the east coast by means of the great river Zambezi.'

He was back at Linyanti in September 1855, nearly 4000 kilometres later. The die was cast: Livingstone was about to walk clear across Africa, from west to east, one of the 19th century's greatest feats of exploration.

There was no way we, in the 21st century, could follow his tracks to Luanda. Although the first hundred kilometres or so would be in peaceful Botswana and Zambia, the rest would take us through central Angola, a country devastated by war, sown with millions of landmines and prowled by the guerrilla armies of Jonas Savimbi's Unita movement.

We sat in Fawlty Towers Backpackers in Livingstone, poring over a map, wondering whether there could be a way, then conceded that the only reasonable direction for us was east. Livingstone had traversed around 43,000 kilometres; we reckoned there were a few we would have to skip. Livingstone had decided to travel on the north bank of the Zambezi under the impression that Tete, the farthest Portuguese inland station, was on that side (it wasn't). In November 1855, accompanied by Chief Sekeletu of the Makololo, the missionary headed downriver by canoe. Soon after leaving, the chief asked Livingstone: 'Have you smoke that thunders in your country?' He pointed at columns of vapour rising into the blue sky, their summits seeming to mingle with the clouds. Livingstone soon heard a dull roar, and the boatmen brought them to an island in the middle of the river 'on the very edge of the lip over which the water rolls'. They stood and stared at the boiling torrent below them.

In his travels, the missionary almost always noted and respected local names of rivers, mountains and areas. But when he beheld the great falls on the Zambezi, he was so awestruck he departed from this policy and named them after the Queen of England.

Victoria Falls remains one of the natural wonders of Africa. Today, when it is almost a clichéd destination, standing at the lip of the great chasm watching millions of tons of water thundering into the gorge is still a moment of profound wonder. We got ourselves happily drenched as we crossed over Knife Edge Bridge to the very lip of the gorge, where we watched circular rainbows ghosting through the spray, then headed back to town for a night of revelry and good company at Fawlty Towers.

Early next morning we were travelling east on the T1 highway, heading for Chirundu and Lower Zambezi National Park. The countryside was mostly table-flat and cloaked in mopane woodland, but after turning down the A1 south of Lusaka, the road dived into some spectacular hills as it dropped into the Zambezi Valley beside the Kafue Gorge. This was Batoka country.

Livingstone was a marvellously perceptive ethnographer and naturalist. Plodding down the river, he took time – sometimes days – to question people about their customs, or to note species, often drawing them with meticulous care. When he met the Batoka at the Kafue, however, their lack of front teeth startled him. They had them knocked out at puberty, and considered anyone with front teeth to be ugly. When he asked the reason, the Batoka told him 'they wished to look like oxen, and not like zebras'. The answer left him even more puzzled. By the time we arrived, front teeth were back in fashion; maybe something to do with the absence of zebras.

As Livingstone dropped down the valley, he speculated on the food value of maneko fruit and the seeds of *nux vomica*; watched in amazement as mopane trees folded their leaves, presenting the smallest surface to harsh sunlight; experimented with the navigation abilities of soldier ants, concluding (quite rightly) that they tracked by scent. He watched 'plasterer' wasps stunning creatures in which to lay their eggs; filled pages of his diary on the environmental value of termites; noted the diets of oxpeckers; turned 'with a feeling of sickness unrelieved by the recollection that the ivory was mine' when his men killed an elephant. He followed honey guides to see if they really led to honey (they did – 114 times to hives and only once to an elephant).

His legendary cool saved him when a band brandishing battle-axes threatened his party. A warrior, howling and in a frenzy – his eyes protruding, his lips covered in foam – advanced on the missionary, axe raised. 'I felt some alarm,' he wrote, 'but disguised it from the spectators, and kept a sharp lookout on the battle axe. After my courage had been suffi-ciently tested, I beckoned to the others to remove him … I should like to have felt his pulse to ascertain whether the violent trembling were not feigned.'

As Livingstone had done 160 years before, we topped a low range of hills and beheld a glorious view. Below us was the Kafue, wending its way over a forest-clad plain to its confluence with the Zambezi. In Livingstone's day it was an even greater spectacle, with more game than he had seen anywhere else in Africa.

'Hundreds of buffaloes and zebras grazed on the open spaces, and beneath the trees stood lordly elephants feeding majestically. The number of animals was quite astonishing. I wished I could have photographed a scene so seldom beheld, and which is destined, as guns increase, to pass away from Earth.'

The great herds have, indeed, passed away, but a few kilometres outside Chirundu we came across wildness of a more modern type. Chirundu is a border town (Zimbabwe's just across the Otto Beit Bridge) and seemingly every long-haul truck and trailer in Zambia was parked along the road and in the surrounding fields.

Consignments were being checked, rechecked and squabbled over. Darting between the iron monsters were harassed-looking officials, police with guns, fruit sellers, water carriers and flocks of young, pretty prostitutes. The entire process seemed out of control, a madness of paperwork, chrome rigs and belching exhausts. We hopped between the monsters, defied a gun-toting man in brown fatigues, and dived down a heavily rutted track with a signpost to Gwabi Lodge.

The lodge, the longest-established in the area and built on the banks of the Kafue, proved to be a haven of peace and beauty. We roasted potatoes and butternuts on an open fire and sipped sherry, watching the sun sink across the silver water.

A few hundred metres down a dusty track the following morning we arrived at the Kafue crossing, serviced by an ancient-looking pontoon winched back and forth by sweating men in tattered shirts. Two vehicles at a time and much effort: what did they do in the busy season? We looked in at Mvuu Lodge, a pleasant place indeed, then continued a bit further to Msaku-Mbezi Lodge where we were to overnight. Just beyond its chalets the Zambezi was sliding past, almost a kilometre wide. On the far bank was Mana Pools National Park in Zimbabwe. The whole lodge vibrated to the harrumphs of hippos and echoed with the cries of fish eagles.

I did a Livingstone-type experiment and found the river was moving at 6.5 kilometres an hour. Then we cracked open beers and let the peace of the place wash over us.

The villages along this section of the river have probably changed little from when Livingstone came exploring. Rough mud walls held up steep, ragged thatch roofs; woven grain stores were propped on rickety poles to keep supplies out of reach of rats, chickens, cows and damp; people sat round open fires cooking; everywhere children ran naked; tatty chickens pecked at the bare, swept earth between the huts.

In the fields were even more precarious pole towers topped with platforms where young-sters sat, tins and sticks at the ready to chase elephants and baboons from the crops. The only evidence of the present century was bright yellow plastic buckets and an occasional long-handled well pump where women gathered to gossip, laugh and sit round simply being in that slow, tension-free way characteristic of Africa.

On a later detour we drove along a dusty road to Feira, downstream from the Lower Zambezi National Park, at the confluence of the Zambezi and Luangwa rivers. Livingstone arrived at the same spot and thanked God 'for His great mercies in helping us thus far'.

There he discovered the remains of a stone church, a broken bell with the letters IHS and a cross, but no date. Across the Luangwa at Zumbo were several ruined houses, and he speculated they might have belonged to Portuguese missionaries or slavers. We parked

under a huge fig tree at about the point he'd have crossed the Luangwa and watched men in dugout canoes catching tiger fish. Backtracking upriver to Chirundu, we passed the scruffy Nyambadwe Hotel, which had a huge billboard on its side reading 'Welcome to Maximum country. Use it, your life depends on it'. We puzzled over the sign for a while, then realised that Maximum was a local brand of condom.

There is no road down the Zambezi between Chirundu and Tete, so we decided to detour through a politically tense Zimbabwe. The country had run out of fuel (and the rule of law), so we filled up at the border, blessed our long-range tanks and hoped we would not meet any marauding 'war veterans' as we motored down a practically empty road to Harare.

Zimbabwe's capital city is still a beautiful place but, in the crazy, tightening political grip of the country's ageing president, it seemed to be unravelling before our eyes. It was depressing.

We left Harare in wraiths of early morning mist and drove through beautiful, tree-lined avenues and then past neat farms along Enterprise Road. Our destination was Tete in Mozambique. In the misty softness the countryside was mysterious and beautiful. Great granite rocks and huge whalebacks towered over mopane and msasa woodland. The small, neat villages had only bright red tomatoes to sell.

Beyond the scruffy border post was wild Africa – virtually people-free baobab country. Mozambican villages, when they appeared, were just poles and rudimentary thatch, nothing more. As we approached Tete the terrain became drier, tree density thinned and goats multiplied. By the time we rolled into the town, the countryside seemed tired and the people had a strange, uninterested look about them.

The town had been, for many years, the marshalling point for captives dragged down the river by Portuguese slavers. A century of slavery, followed by harsh colonialism and civil war, had left its mark. The once-grand buildings were crumbling, the fort was in ruins and seemed to serve as the local toilet, the only working diesel pump broke as we queued, the bank tried to overcharge (massively) for cashing a traveller's cheque, few people met our eyes, none smiled. Tete, in a word, was the pits. We overnighted in a questionable backpacker joint with filthy toilets and the clatter of noisy overlanders, then fled west up a good tar road to Cahora Bassa.

Livingstone's route to Tete had been more direct. Several days downriver from the Luangwa River his party had been threatened by warriors under Chief Mpende. The missionary roasted an ox and sent a hind leg to the chief. Mpende responded with friendship, saying a Mozunga (Portuguese), his enemy, would never have done such a thing. 'All the slaves of Tete are our children,' he told Livingstone. 'The Bazunga have made a town at our expense.' The chief lent them canoes to cross to the south bank, where Livingstone had been told the tribes were friendlier. Several years later he would regret this decision.

Travelling southeast through forests, he was amazed at the 'hum of insect joy' all about. 'The universality of organic life', he told his diary, 'seems like a mantle of happy existence encircling the world.' Of the birds he exclaimed: 'These African birds have not been wanting in song so much as in poets to sing their praises.'

One night Livingstone's party was surrounded by soldiers, who turned out to be from Tete. As luck would have it, they were friendly. Next morning the soldiers cooked up 'the most refreshing breakfast I ever partook of', then they all headed downriver to the Portuguese settlement. Even then, he found Tete – as we had – 'in a lamentable state'. What he had missed in his more southerly route (with unforeseen consequences) was the terrible Cahora Bassa rapids.

In Tete Livingstone heard talk of a river named Shire, which, it was said, drained a great lake, the Nyanja. He logged this information for future use and journeyed on down the river past Sena to the Zambezi Delta, then northeast to Quelimane on the Indian Ocean coast, which he reached in May 1856.

It was four years since he left Cape Town, three since he had heard from his family in England. He caught a sailing ship to Mauritius, then hitched a ride home to England on the Peninsular and Oriental Steam Ship Company vessel *Candia*. There he received a hero's welcome but found his family impoverished, and his wife, Mary, a virtual alcoholic. During the next two years he was to write his first book, *Missionary Travels and Researches in South Africa*, and undertake countless speaking tours. But, in 1858, Africa would again beckon.

We more modern travellers revelled in the deep gorges and wild mountains Livingstone had initially missed. Following good advice, we'd headed up to Cahora Bassa where we checked into Ugezi Tiger Lodge with its hot showers, cold beer and elegant sophistication which, after Tete, was balm to our dusty souls. It's run by Willie Beeton and you couldn't find a finer base from which to explore the great dam. We spent a day cruising the flooded valleys in a powerboat, transfixed by the sheer rocky sides of the gorges.

That evening we met a Portuguese professional hunter, Rui Rebocho, still sweating from a bout of malaria. Did he know where Mary Livingstone's grave was? He thought it might be at Lacerdonia, but to get there would require a huge detour, down to Gondola – almost to Beira – then up past Gorongoza Park to Caia on the Zambezi. The condition of the roads? 'Bad,' he said. 'Everywhere in Mozambique, bad.'

From there we'd need to hop on a river ferry (if it was running), then travel to Quelimane and inland to Blantyre – an awful-sounding dogleg – to get to southern Malawi and the Shire River. How long would it take? 'Five days, maybe more.'

That night I awoke in the small hours with a great state of anxiety, cowed by the precariousness of our position. Would we get lost? Would there be diesel? What if our Colt broke down far from help? Was the ferry running? Were the locals friendly? Was it irresponsible to put my wife, Patricia, through this?

Dawn, as it usually does, sizzled away most of my anxiety. We packed, bade Ugezi Lodge farewell, and headed down the road towards Beira.

In 1862, desperate to be back in the Africa she loved, Mary Livingstone had joined her husband on the Zambezi. She didn't last four months. As we hummed down the endless, empty road it struck me there was a certain madness travelling an extra 2000 kilometres to search for the grave of someone who died of malaria and probably alcohol poisoning 139 years ago.

Not far from Mutare – but still in Mozambique – we stopped beside a lake named Chicamba and found Pip Thornycroft's chalets, restaurant and camping ground. It was a charming spot and, beers in hand, we watched the sun set over Zimbabwe's Eastern Highlands. Then we cooked some brown rice with a packet of chicken soup, threw in a handful of crushed garlic to ward off mosquitoes, and opened a tin of salmon. Camp cuisine at its best.

Next morning we filled up at Chimoio – a fair-sized town – then turned north towards Gorongoza National Park along the worst road we'd been on so far. It had once been tarred, but was so holed and rutted that our average speed for the next 60 kilometres was around 15 kilometres an hour. Beyond the park we found that Grinaker Construction, a South African firm, was pushing a new road to the Zambezi, so we had a section of fine tar, then well-graded diversions.

At one point there was a sign announcing 'Road closed. No through road to Caia.' That was where we had planned to cross the Zambezi: to go back would mean a three-day detour. We were dumbstruck. Just then a man driving a tractor puttered up, waved his hand airily and pronounced the road open. And he was right.

Near Caia we came across a well-kitted party of 21st-century 'Voortrekkers' with engineer Ockie Müller in the lead wagon: a smart Toyota Land Cruiser. They took us in, headed for a wild but wonderful camp site Ockie had organised, formed their shiny 4x4s into a laager and soon had coffee and fire bread on the go. They were the most efficient, fun-loving adventurers we'd ever met. Beers in hand, we toasted all travellers.

Ockie looked startled when we told him we were heading to Quelimane en route to Malawi. 'You don't have to do that,' he said. 'Just drive across the Dona Ana Rail Bridge at Sena and straight up the Shire River to Blantyre.'

'The trains?' we asked.

'The tracks were blown up ages ago. The bridge is fine.'

First, though, there was the matter of Mary's grave. We headed downriver into the Zambezi Delta through really wild country towards what our map told us was Lacerdonia. What we found was a faded marker with the town's name on it and a rusting Caltex sign sticking through some foliage. War had destroyed the village and the impenetrable forest had swallowed what was left. Could the grave be there? If it was, how would we begin searching for it?

Raising the ghosts of a doomed adventure

From where we sat in the Zambezi Delta, it was obvious David Livingstone's Zambezia Expedition was bound for disaster. The Cahora Bassa rapids were impassable, the shifting sandbars of the Zambezi were treacherous and, in summer, the place would be a malarial hellhole.

Even today the delta's a wild place. It's beautiful, with spectacular sand forests and flood-plains, to be sure, but awfully far away from help if trouble strikes. And the 1858 expedition had nothing but trouble, not the least being the death of Mary Livingstone.

There was clearly no longer a place named Lacerdonia, so we pressed on downriver until we encountered an official-looking building with the word 'Shupanga' on it. We never figured out what the scruffy office was for, and the village – if it was one – was not on any map we had. But the name rang a bell. Livingstone had offloaded supplies at this spot on the river. I dug in Livingstone's Shire Journal and there it was: 'Mary', wrote Livingstone, 'rests by the large baobab tree at Shupanga.'

Down a track we found a wrecked, roofless Portuguese mission amid thousands of tents: the place was a refugee camp for peasants displaced by the Zambezi floods. We drove through rows of World Vision and Spanish Red Cross shelters while Patricia tried to remember the Portuguese for 'colonial cemetery'. When it came to her, we asked a man if there was one. There was, he said, and jumped aboard to show us.

The gate and fence surrounding it were virtually hidden by bushes. There was no baobab tree. He took us to some relatively new graves and pointed hopefully. No, we shook our heads, these were too recent. Was there a 'grande' grave? Then we spotted a cross atop a cast-iron gravestone. I ploughed my way through waist-high grass to read the inscription, but it was in Portuguese so I turned away.

'Wait!' yelled Patricia, who was just behind me. 'There's the name Mary Moffat.' We cleared the brambles and, sure enough, it was Mary's grave. An English inscription was on the back. It was in a terrible state of disrepair, with part of the headstone broken off. The surrounding chain had come adrift and voracious foliage was dismembering the cementwork. I'll be surprised if it lasts another year.

We sat beside it, sadly, thinking of the pain and probably guilt that David must have felt standing there so many years ago. Sad, also, because while her husband was buried in Westminster Abbey, Mary should lie under such a neglected pile of rubble in a forgotten village amid dirt-poor refugees. In death, as in life, she had a raw deal.

We backtracked to Caia, then further upriver to Sena, heading for the Dona Ana Bridge. Our map flagged it as 'the longest railway bridge in Africa'. On the way there we nearly had a head-on with a clapped-out Land-Rover full of people and chickens. The driver, on the wrong side of the road, swerved across our path and the Landy dived into a ditch, chickens flying. Miraculously, nobody was hurt. We pulled it out with our snatch rope, but then the men got threatening so we jumped into our Colt and fled.

The bridge was startlingly long, somewhat rickety, no longer a rail bridge but a thrilling ride. Beyond it the road simply disappeared, replaced by what can be described only as a sled path. We were running late and wouldn't make the Malawian border, so we pulled into a village and asked if we could overnight.

We were offered the schoolyard, and soon maybe 200 children and not a few adults were pressing round our vehicle. It was unnerving and the hubbub was deafening. I can now imagine what a sensation Dr L and his party must have made in such villages. I took some flash photos and every time the bulb popped 200 young voices cheered. If we sat in the van, faces would press up against the windows. It took at least three hours for the crowd to thin out, and by then we were exhausted from simply being stared at.

A young man named Farucky K'Kaonza, seeing our distress, shooed away the children and invited us into his hut. We broke out some Zambezi beers and discussed the recent floods and the problem of refugees. He and his young wife were desperately poor.

That night we slept to the sound of goats bleating, cows lowing, dogs yapping and people chatting, laughing and, eventually, snoring.

Next morning we fled before the children awoke. The road to the Malawian border at Villa Nova was lined with ragged poverty. The only clue to the frontier was a pole across the road and a sleepy moneychanger flapping dirty kwacha notes at us. Then we noticed a ruin of what must once have been a fine customs house – bombed, we later discovered, by Renamo soldiers.

The immigration official was even sleepier than the moneychanger and was housed in a grass-walled shed. He stamped our passports hard because there was no ink left in the stamp pad, and directed us to another grass shed where the customs man puzzled over our carnet before handing back all our papers and shooing us over the border.

The Malawian post was, by comparison, all spit and polish. A smart official handed us forms, stamped our passports, dealt with the carnet, offered us brochures about his country and wished us a pleasant stay. After the poverty of Mozambique, Malawi was a relief. The people were peasant-poor, but not dog-poor. They smiled, waved, trotted by in bright dresses or pedalled shiny bicycles loaded beyond belief.

We dodged pedestrians along the road beside the Shire River to Chikwawa and the Murchison Cataracts, which had stopped Livingstone's paddle steamer. Then we ground up a steep, winding road into the Shire Highlands. The views of the Shire and Zambezi valleys were dreamy.

Blantyre, nestled in the highlands, is a busy but pleasant town with some good restaurants and Doogles Backpackers, which is the pub to gather at sunset to drink, eat and meet fellow travellers and interesting locals. After gathering our strength in the home of some new friends we'd made at Cahora Bassa, we headed up the road to Zomba Plateau.

If the roads of Malawi are any indication of population density, the country is filled to capacity. We were on the lookout for a stretch of road without people but never found one. An hour or so out of Blantyre, Zomba loomed – an impressive 2000-metre-high plateau muscling out of the Rift Valley floor.

Zomba town at its feet is a delightful, tree-filled place, which was once described in traveller's dispatches as 'the most beautiful capital in the Commonwealth'. It's no longer a capital, but there's a fine state house and a first-class bakery where we bought some fresh rolls. Then we wound our way up the mountain past clumps of dragon trees. The views over the plain were magnificent, blurring through soft purples to merge with the sky.

There's an inviting-looking hotel atop the mountain, but its kitchen had burned down and it was closed. Along the road were hawkers selling huge quartz crystals for ridiculously low prices, and men pushing bicycles piled metres high with firewood.

From Zomba we headed up the Shire again, turning east at the village of Liwonde, then up into the national park of the same name. Liwonde's not endowed with large animal

populations – though there's no shortage of giant crocs in the Shire, and elephants along the shore. But it has a special quality, an attractiveness which is beguiling. Stark euphorbias, tall doum palms and bright yellow fever trees attended sage baobabs, huge and small. Along the river, all manner of creatures rustled in the reed beds.

We picked our way through the park to Mvuu Lodge, a luxurious place where you can sleep to the grunting of hippos and the snapping of crocs. When we'd shaken the dust off our boots, we puttered upriver in the lodge boat, watching elephants swimming between reed beds, yawning hippos and fish-eyed saurians cruising the shallows. If you fell out of the boat there, you'd be instant croc protein.

Mvuu provided some unaccustomed luxury: hot shower, flush toilet, courtesy soaps, flowers on the pillows and excellent food. We felt we'd earned it.

Our next destination was Cape Maclear, which Livingstone named after his friend, the Astronomer Royal, Thomas Maclear. It's a fishing village among the hills which are scattered round Lake Malawi's southern edge. It was 'discovered' by the outside world, and now a dive school, Kayak Africa and several backpacker joints have shouldered in among the huts. There the amiable Juri Schoeman kitted us out with kayaks, provided a guide, and shooed us out across the sparkling lake to Domwe Island, where Kayak Africa has the sort of camp most people only imagine in their dreams.

Under Livingstone's direction, a four-oared rowing boat was carried above the Murchison Cataracts and the party rowed up the Shire, watching the banks get further and further apart. The excitement of that inveterate seeker of African waterways must have been unbounded when he realised he was rowing into the southern end of a vast lake.

With a party of bearers on the shore and Livingstone in the boat, they proceeded north until the bearers – horrified by the burned villages littered with skeletons and decimated, starving people – refused to go any further. It was Livingstone's first contact with large-scale slavery, and it was to set the course of the rest of his life. Only commerce could kill the horror trade in humans, he decided, so colonisation was therefore the Crown's moral duty.

That evening we sat at the edge of Livingstone's lake, watching the sun sink over Mumbo Island. Livingstone was a man who seldom recorded his feelings, and the dead bodies bobbing in the lake would have tempered his elation. Here was a paradise polluted by the hell of slavery.

From Cape Maclear we took a rough, shore-hugging road round the lake to the M5 highway, then headed northwards up the lake to Nkhotakota. For much of the 19th century, this was the largest slave market on Lake Nyasa (now Lake Malawi); the terminus from where up to 20,000 slaves a year were shipped across the lake in dhows to the northern shore, then marched to Kilwa Kivinje on the coast.

The trade in humans at Nkhotakota was established by an Arab half-caste named Jumbe, who founded a dynasty lasting well into the 20th century. When Livingstone reached the village in 1861 he described it as 'an abode of lawlessness and bloodshed ... literally strewed with human bones and putrid bodies'.

When he returned in 1863, he sat under a giant fig tree and tried, unsuccessfully, to convince Jumbe to abandon slavery. The tree still stands in the grounds of St Ann's Mission Hospital. The ragged little town, with its collapsed jetty and unpainted shops, shows little evidence of its bloody past. With the assistance of the hospital superintendent we found the wall of Jumbe's mosque, the beach from which the slaves were loaded and a large, tree-shaded area where slaves were marshalled, graded and sent off to unknowable futures – and often death.

Just outside Nkhotakota we tracked down Sani Beach Resort, owned by Andy and Cathy Olivier, an idyllic place where we watched fishermen hauling nets and catching precious little. Next morning we headed south to Salima, then picked up Livingstone's trail through Lilongwe to the Zambian border.

We were now on the route of Livingstone's most spectacular, and ultimately crazy, journey. It was a venture in which he would fail utterly, yet the world would revere him for it. For us it promised the badlands of western Tanzania and the great unknown. But first there was the matter of an explorer's heart buried beneath a tree beside the Bangweulu Swamps.

Disaster on the Zambezi

When David Livingstone arrived in England early in 1856 after travelling from Luanda to Quelimane, he received a measure of praise and adulation which, even today, seems excessive.

In church, if he was recognised, the service would break up in chaos, with people clambering over pews to try to shake his hand. In London he had to be careful not to be mobbed: on one occasion he narrowly escaped being crushed by a large crowd in Regent Street. He was granted the freedom of half a dozen cities. The Royal Geographical Society gave him their gold medal, as did most similar organisations on the Continent. He was granted a private meeting with Queen Victoria. His book, *Missionary Travels and Researches in South Africa*, sold 70,000 copies. It made him a rich man.

His transcontinental journey seemed to his contemporaries to be a feat comparable in modern terms with a landing on Mars. The commonly held view of south-central Africa was that of a useless area not unlike the Sahara. But, as one journalist put it, Livingstone found himself 'in a high country, full of fruit trees, abounding in shade, watered by a perfect network of rivers'.

The Livingstone myth was in the making. 'Seldom have savage nations met with the representative of English Civilization in such hope,' wrote another journalist. 'He came not for conquest or for gold, but for the love of his fellow men.' That he was Scottish was ignored.

Livingstone did not see fit to contradict these views, though Mary might have seen things differently. To counter the scourge of slavery and to free England from dependency on American cotton, he had developed a plan and needed all the support he could garner. South-central Africa needed to be colonised, and a start would be the Batoka Plateau (in present-day Zambia).

He could, he reasoned, enter the mouth of the Zambezi with a shallow-draught boat. He would reach Tete as quickly as possible and then proceed to the Cahora Bassa rapids 'to discover whether the launch would be able to steam up there when the river is high'. Once he had 'proved' the Zambezi to be navigable, the next step would be to head upstream to the plateau, erect an iron house as the centre for stores, and begin agricultural experiments aimed at proving that enough sugar and cotton could be grown to make the area a commercial paradise. All this, he thought, would take but two years.

It was a breathtakingly simple schedule. The mood of the times did the rest: he got his boat, his iron house, £500 a year from the British Government plus £50,000 to fit out the expedition. He also attracted some excellent and skilled men (including the artist Thomas Baines and John Kirk, the future governor of Zanzibar) and a questionable one: his brother Charles. Shortly before the Zambezi Expedition set sail from Liverpool on 10 March 1858, Livingstone was given the title of Her Majesty's Consul of Quelimane.

On the ship out, Mary, who insisted on coming with her husband, found she was pregnant again. She was dispatched up to Kuruman to have the baby, then back to Scotland, which she hated. She would not see Livingstone for another four years.

The steamship *Pearl* anchored off the Zambezi sandbars on 14 May. The vessel was being pounded by surf and it was soon clear that the plan to take it up to Tete would have to be abandoned. The *Ma-Robert*, a small paddle steamer shipped in pieces, was hastily bolted together and given the job. It was soon obvious it was a dubious vessel: it required prodigious quantities of wood, its draught was too deep and it had to be winched across the bars and sand flats (three days aground was not uncommon). Its plates were too thin, eventually springing hundreds of leaks, and its engine, Livingstone observed, was 'evidently made to grind coffee in a shop window'.

It would be surprising if the tempers of the men, slogging under a blazing sun and plagued by mosquitoes, ticks and tropical ulcers, had not frayed. Livingstone, a lone traveller by nature, either refused to take a lead, or fired men whom his pompous brother, Charles, disliked. Soon morale was at rock bottom.

It took six months of ferrying to get all the supplies to Shupanga, Sena and Tete. Then it was time to investigate the 'small rapid' at Cahora Bassa which Livingstone had missed on his previous trip down the river. He set off with Kirk and they discovered a boiling cascade. To Kirk it was obvious that no vessel could pass upstream, but Livingstone hedged: maybe when the river was flooded? He even wrote a dispatch to the British Foreign Secretary that 'a steamer of light draught would pass the rapids without difficulty when the river is in full flood'. Kirk, who saw the dispatch, was appalled. But finally it sank in: the boiling rapids were not navigable. 'Things look dark for our enterprise,' Livingstone wrote in his diary.

Worse news was to follow. In the wake of Livingstone's talks in England, an enterprise had been formed to send out a mission to the Batoka Plateau. The so-called Universities Mission was now on its way, headed by a bishop.

Livingstone needed a plan, and fast. The solution was the Shire River. It flowed into the Zambezi roughly 160 kilometres from the coast and he hoped it was navigable.

By the time the Universities Mission arrived, Livingstone had explored the Shire and seen the Shire Highlands. He also realised the river emerged from a great lake, the Nyasa (now Lake Malawi). Here, he decided, was a fine place for a mission. There were some concerns, however, which he shared only with his diary. Slaving was rife in the area and the tribes were 'stirred up'. So were the members of his party. Baines had been fired for 'pilfering stores' (a charge never substantiated), as had several other men for various perceived misdemeanours.

When the missionaries arrived, the *Ma-Robert* was leaking like a colander. Livingstone ordered two more steamers (one he paid for himself) and, surprisingly, *Pioneer* and *Lady Nyasa* were eventually delivered. With them came Mary, having left her youngest child with relatives.

The Universities Mission was a disaster from beginning to end. The party had to wait months for the rainy season in order to get up the Shire. They were involved in skirmishes with slavers, and many, including Bishop Mackenzie, died of malaria. The mission was eventually abandoned.

Four months after Mary arrived she fell ill with fever. Livingstone was concerned, but became really worried when quinine had no healing effect. Drink had lowered her resistance. On 27 April 1862 her breathing became laboured. Livingstone took her in his arms and choked: 'My dearie, my dearie, you are going to leave me … are you resting on Jesus?' Soon afterwards she died and was buried in the grave we had just rediscovered under a massive baobab tree. She was 41.

After Mary's death Livingstone became less harsh with his men, but more obsessive and inflexible in his determination to push himself to the limit. In his diary he wrote percep-tively: 'Am I a martyr to my own cause? I begin to think that I may not live to see success.'

He decided to explore the Rovuma River (now the border between Mozambique and Tanzania). It took months of dragging the steamer over mud and sand. The trip was clearly ridiculous. Kirk wrote in his journal: 'I can come to no other conclusion than that Dr L is out of his mind … his head is not of the ordinary construction but what is termed cracked.'

But Livingstone sought, as ever, to allay his doubts through action. Before Mary died he had walked back to Linyanti in present-day Namibia and back. He returned from the Rovuma to explore Lake Nyasa. The Shire region was in the grip of a famine and racked by slavery. Dead, bloated bodies floated downstream and became entangled in the paddle wheels (in one week he counted 19). It was a horrific trip. He then walked as far as the present South Luangwa National Park in Zambia. But news of the disastrous expedition got back to London. The Zambezi had not been navigated, a dozen lives had been lost and there was little to show for the £50,000 spent. The expedition was deemed a failure and recalled. Five years of slog were over.

But Livingstone was not quite done with adventure. He decided the best place to sell his riverboat, *Lady Nyasa*, would be in Bombay. The 12-metre vessel was a river craft, he was no sailor and the monsoons were due. But he set off for Zanzibar with an African crew which had never been to sea before, then headed out across the Indian Ocean. It took him 45 days, but he made it. The monsoons broke the next day. He sold his boat and hitched a ship home.

When he reached London in July 1864 there were no banquets or official receptions. The powerful and the public had lost interest. 'All my work', he wrote, 'seems in vain.'

The road to Bagamoyo

Our final journey, we were told, was probably impossible. The plan was to drive from Malawi straight to the Great North Road in Zambia – between North and South Luangwa parks – then up the eastern shore of Lake Tanganyika to Ujiji. From there we planned to head for the old slaving capital of Tabora in central Tanganyika, then on to Bagamoyo on the coast.

We could find nobody who'd done the trip. A United Nations website advisory claimed there were bandits along the roads near Ujiji. There was a war going on just across the lake in Congo, and huge refugee movement was causing problems along the road skirting the Burundian border – a road we'd have to take. Before leaving we'd cast the net wide among all the travellers and overland agents we could muster and none had ever heard of anyone getting to Tabora.

By the time we reached Nkhotakota on Lake Malawi, however, we were in a very 'can do' mood. Our Colt was performing magnificently; we were having fun and, well, that's the way David Livingstone went. So early one morning we bid farewell to the Lake of Stars and set off on the impossible journey.

We overnighted at a beautiful site just inside Zambia named Yellow Chicken Camp – lawns to park on, good food and a pub – then negotiated the appalling road between Chipata and South Luangwa National Park.

ON 27th JUNE 1857 BURTON AND SPEKE SET OFF FROM KAOLE NEAR THIS SITE ON THEIR EXPEDITION TO LAKE TANGANYIKA

We pulled into Flat Dogs Camp, only to discover that the flooding Munyamadzi River would prevent us from reaching the Great North Road (T2) that way. That meant backtracking down the bad road we'd just negotiated, then a detour of more than 1000 kilometres via Lusaka. We did some washing on the banks of the Luangwa River, turned in early and were gone before sunrise.

The detour was long, but Zambia is beautiful, with some fine overnight stops along the way – Bridge Camp on the southern Luangwa River being one, another being Forest Inn near Mkushi on the Great North Road. Along the way we popped in at the farm of David and Christine Moffat. David's a descendant of Robert Moffat, Livingstone's father-in-law. They're good people, still doing missionary-type work among the locals. Some way beyond the farm we turned northwest onto the D235 and pulled into Kasanka National Park, a privately run place created as a trust by former hunter David Lloyd. It's just south of the Bangweulu Swamps where David Livingstone died.

Next morning we went in search of the grave. The road went by way of Chief Chitambo's palace and we popped in to pay our respects. There was a sign which read 'Off the Bicycle, Take Off Your Hat'. As we weren't on a bicycle we rolled into the palace, but the chief was out. So we headed up an obscure track through villages and finally arrived at a peaceful avenue of shady trees, at the end of which was a rather graceless concrete tower with a cross on top.

Halfway down the avenue was a simple plaque: 'David Livingstone, traveller, medical missionary died here May 1, 1873. Chitambo's Village.' It was a long way from where Mary died; both had departed this world in lonely, hard-to-find places.

At the village of Mpika we turned off the Great North Road and headed up the M1 to Kasama. For the first 100 kilometres the road was perfect; for the next 100 it was a nightmare of potholes. Eventually a ridge of hills appeared, then a sign announcing 'Kasama, the heart of Northern Zambia'.

We found the warm heart of Kasama to be Thorn Tree Guesthouse, run by Hazel and Ewart Powell. Sitting on their stoep gazing over the plain we'd driven across, we worked out excuses for staying a few days longer. One good reason was a Pygmy rock-art site: moody rocks with strange forest spirits and flying, fish-like humans. I hadn't realised Pygmies did Bushman-type art.

Nobody in Kasama knew whether it was safe or even still possible to drive up Lake Tanganyika to Ujiji. So we rolled up to the border at Mbala – along the last tar road we would see for many thousands of kilometres – with a good deal of trepidation.

The immigration man in Mbala had to be searched for – travellers were clearly not common on that road. From there the road simply went to hell: it looked more like a riverbed.

The track up the lake to Sumbawanga was as bad as it gets. We often had to rely on the GPS to assure us we were on a road at all. It took us four hours to do 130 kilometres. There were no camp sites at Sumbawanga and no obvious hotels, but we finally found our way to the Forestway Country Club. It's run by Amir Mitha and has comfortable rooms plus a friendly bar and restaurant.

Amir's a storehouse of local knowledge and pretty good on the state of the roads. At Forestway we met Stephanie and Mario Ferraz from the Congo – young travellers old beyond their years. Their tales of doing business in that troubled country were harrowing but intriguing.

'Once you've lived in the Congo,' Mario commented, 'there's no place in Africa you're afraid of.'

We drank beer and toasted the mad continent, declaring it the only place to be. They agreed to travel up the lake with us: given the terrible road, the dangers of bandits and the uncertainty of ever reaching Kigoma and Ujiji, I cannot begin to convey the magnanimity of that gesture.

'They are angels from heaven,' Patricia sighed as we turned in for the night.

The road up the lake from Sumbawanga heads midway between Lakes Tanganyika and Rukwa, the latter being an ancient depression where dinosaur eggs have been found. Our track turned northeast into the Katavi National Park, probably the most abandoned reserve in Tanzania. There are places on this planet where humans are not part of the equation, and Katavi is one of them.

For what seemed countless kilometres we drove through magnificent, old miombo woodland. At one point, as we were rounding a curve, a huge, black giraffe confronted us. His coat was so dark we saw only his splotched markings up close. He seemed like something right out of a dream.

Arriving at Katavi's base camp, we found a few uninterested rangers who offered us crude huts at exorbitant prices, so we headed on to Mpanda. The town is not exactly a destination of much distinction: dusty stalls, unpainted shops and, rather surprisingly, a hotel named City Lights. There are gold mines nearby and the town definitely has a Wild West air.

We checked into City Lights (there is no camp site) and sat in the beer garden drinking cold beer to the amplified, distorted cacophony of Tanzanian Television. The showers were cold but the beds were vermin-free and the food perfectly edible.

Next morning we hit the road to Kigoma, the town of which Ujiji is now a suburb – and what a road! It quite rightly has the reputation of a hell run. It's around 300 kilometres and the trip took us ten-and-a-half hours. On the other hand, it's a 4x4 enthusiast's dream – rock climbing, sand scrambling, giant holes and narrow tracks between gaping, flood-scoured gullies.

Near a few huts, dignified on the map with the name Kaloma, a dust-spewing convoy of smart 4x4s appeared, the two in front armed to the teeth. We edged over as they roared past, the logos on the doors identifying them as being from the United Nations, Anglo

American and the Jane Goodall Foundation – off, we discovered, to film chimps for *National Geographic*. The last vehicle rolled to a stop and a man with an Afrikaans accent introduced himself.

'What's with the escort?' I asked.

'Don't you know?' He looked astonished at my ignorance. 'There are bandits on this road!'

We didn't, and set off again hoping the military had scared them off. On his advice we took a short cut at the village of Uvinza along a new road built to service the large Lugufu refugee camp: what a relief! But beyond the camp the road reverted to The Horror. After night had fallen, feeling exhausted from all the banging about, we drove into an avenue of ancient mango trees, Kigoma's main street.

Kigoma is a wonderful village, friendly, bustling with trade and perched on the beautiful, sparkling lakeshore. We overnighted in the grand Kigoma Hilltop Hotel, but moved out the next day. It was expensive and strangely unfriendly. Minesh Joshi, the local manager of Sunset Tours, offered us a room in his home, and we were spoiled with his delicious home cooking. Minesh has a heart of gold and can organise anything. He lined up contacts all the way to Dar es Salaam. Next day we bumped out to Ujiji past countless traders, quaint tearooms and a puzzlingly high number of hairdressing salons (usually spelled 'saloons').

There are several versions of what must be one of the world's most historic handshakes, but Govola Mbinga, the guide at the place where Henry Morton Stanley met Livingstone, tells it best.

'Yivingstone he neary dead man when one he come running crying: "Hear come Yingrish mzungu!" Yivingstone he sit under big mango tree and Stanrey come he say by Yivingstone: "I presume." Mmmm. Dey shakum hands. Shake, shake. Dey meet like thatumm. Stanrey try to persuade Yivingstone to come to Europe mmm. But no, he would not go, nooooo. He go look for Nileumm.'

Livingstone had been lost to the rest of the world for six years when journalist Stanley marched into Ujiji with a long line of porters, a huge store of supplies and the Stars and Stripes flying. He wasn't 'Yingrish', of course, but Welsh – reporting for the *New York Herald* – and had just landed the scoop of a lifetime. It was 10 November 1871.

Today the meeting spot consists of an unattractive stone plinth beneath two mango trees said to have been grafted from the original, which was cut down and sent to London.

Kigoma was a hard place to leave – everyone begged us to stay longer – but we had a deadline. We bid farewell to our guardian angels, Mario and Stephanie, and next morning

made a pre-dawn start up the appalling road to Kasusu. From there it was the dubious run up the Burundian border to Nyakanazi (we had been warned of bandits). It's a road of refugee camps – hundreds of thousands seeking sanctuary from the many wars in the region – but the surface had, mercifully, been graded by aid agencies. Every few kilometres we'd come across a new white Toyota Land Cruiser with 'Red Cross', 'Oxfam' or 'UN' emblazoned on the doors. The humanitarians had expensive tastes.

Surprisingly, from Nyakanazi all the way to Kahama, the road was tarred. In Kahama we found a delightful Dutch-owned rest house run by a large, happy woman named Rose. We sluiced the dust off in a hot shower and jumped into a large double bed under a diaphanous mosquito net. A thumping storm ended the day and sent the rock doves outside into paroxysms of blissful pleasure.

Early next morning there was a difficult decision to make. Some 200 kilometres south, down an undoubtedly awful road, lay Tabora, where Livingstone had recuperated after Stanley trundled off to fame and fortune. The rain wouldn't have improved the road, we were travel-weary and the coast beckoned. Right then, Tabora seemed to be at the end of the earth. We didn't make the decision until the turnoff appeared at Nzega. Then we just turned south to Tabora.

The road *was* awful, but when the town appeared it was in a virtual forest of mango trees (a sure sign of Arab slavers) and one of the most attractive we'd visited. It was aclutter with small stalls selling bright cloth and crammed with women wearing it. A friendly policeman directed us to the Wilco Hotel, which had a tree-covered courtyard, a clean restaurant and quaint little rooms around a second, flower-filled square. At sundown the call of a muezzin rang across the ancient buildings.

On the recommendation of Minesh Joshi in Kigoma we contacted a friend of his, Raju Lodhia, who came round and offered to show us his town. First stop was the Arab slaver's house where Livingstone had spent, by his account, many pleasureful months. It was some five kilometres out of town, with no signposts. There is a small Livingstone museum in one room, with bits of memorabilia.

Wilco served a fine vegetable curry and Raju joined us to debate the best way to get to Dodoma on our way to the coast. We could backtrack to Nzega, head for Singida, then turn south to Dodoma: a three-day journey. An alternative was a track beside the railway line between Tabora and Dodoma: less than a day, but dangerous. Raju advised us against it: bridges down, wild country, no people at all. Next day we asked a man at the garage if the track was open. Sure, he said, a Land-Rover came that way a month ago. 'But if you break down....'

It's hard to explain exactly why, but we opted for the track. By then we trusted the Colt completely and figured we'd call on all the angels and jinn to do the rest.

We left, as usual, before dawn and were soon in high, beautiful miombo woodland. The few people we came across fled as we approached: were there still slaving caravans?

Every bridge – deep culverts really – had washed away but we skirted them with little difficulty until we came to a swamp. It was soggy, black-cotton mud and we'd need to cross about 30 metres of it. With 100 kilometres of track behind us, and three days of detour after that, forward seemed the only option. I backed up as far as I could and roared towards the morass.

The Colt plunged in, flinging mud in every direction including onto the windscreen. It bucked and slithered but held direction and finally leapt up onto a bank of hard ground. We got out and looked at the 4x4. It was an unrecognisable block of pig-swill-smelling mud. The windscreen wipers did what they could and we were soon back on the track to Dodoma. If we'd got stuck, would we have had to wait a month for help, or maybe more? It didn't bear thinking about.

Of Dodoma what can I say? Give it a miss. Its only value is that the tar road to the coast begins there. Some ten hours after leaving Tabora we nosed into the afternoon traffic of Dar es Salaam.

::

There's a restaurant in Dar named Bar es Salaam. Its décor is Malian, its ceiling is silky white drapes, it's managed by William and serviced by the beautiful, dusky Deborah. The food is cooked with consummate skill, the beer is cold, the music is the best from Africa and on Thursdays and Saturdays it's live.

Maybe it's an extraordinary place, maybe it's not, but after 13,000 kilometres of roads mostly from hell we were unable to judge. We sat grinning at each other saying things like:

'This is *so* cool!' The next night we were back for more of the same. The beer, if anything, tasted even better. Civilisation has some definite advantages.

Livingstone had no such luck. When he died, his faithful bearers, Susi and Chumah, buried his entrails, dried his body and carried it more than 3000 kilometres to Bagamoyo on the coast – an extraordinary feat. On 24 February 1874 they entered the compound of the Holy Ghost Fathers and deposited it at the door of the church. There they stood in reverent silence until one of the fathers appeared. Susi stepped forward and said 'Mwili wa Dauid' (The body of David).

We motored up the road to Bagamoyo to find the church – part of it still stands, as does the avenue of trees down which Livingstone's body was carried to a British ship for transport to Zanzibar, then London. Bagamoyo is a scruffy but atmospheric village, a crumbling version of Stone Town on Zanzibar Island. Next day we boarded a ferry for Zanzibar to visit the house where Livingstone stayed, and the British consulate building where his body had lain.

Stone Town is surely one of the wonders of Africa. Every building creaks with history. Livingstone walked these streets, as did Stanley, Burton, Speke and almost every other African explorer south of the Sahara.

We booked into the beautiful Dhow Palace – a hotel so gorgeous it was like checking into a fantasy – and shook the dust of mainland Africa from our boots. We would fly back south. Livingstone's body was transported north to London and its final resting place.

The final journey

When Livingstone reached London in July 1864, following the disastrous Zambezi Expedition, there were no banquets and official receptions as there had been in 1856.

The Foreign Secretary, Lord Russell, told him that if he intended to return to Africa the government would pay him no more than £500 towards the trip. No expedition could be mounted for less than £2000, and he was aware that Russell knew that. Livingstone left his office trembling with anger and wounded pride.

He spent some time with his neglected family and began writing *A Narrative of an Expedition to the Zambezi and its Tributaries*.

During this time he became aware of the fateful meeting in Bath where a heated debate was expected to take place between Richard Burton and John Speke on the probable location of the source of the Nile. Speke never made the meeting, having shot himself while out hunting. There was talk of suicide.

The Nile controversy fired Livingstone's interest and would change the course of his life. He decided that the river's source probably lay to the southwest of Lake Tanganyika (it doesn't – Speke was correct: it issues from Lake Victoria). Finding the Nile's source, he told a friend, would 'enable me to open my mouth with power among men'.

His ally in the Royal Geographical Society, Sir Roderick Murchison, got the society to invite Livingstone to return to Africa to clear up the mystery. An old university friend, the inventor of paraffin, James Young, offered him £1000. In 1866, with meagre funds and a flawed reputation, he sailed for Zanzibar on a trip which would end in glorious martyrdom.

After the HMS *Penguin* dropped Livingstone and his party at Rovuma Bay on 19 March, only one white man would see the missionary alive again. To his party of 35 porters – some of whom were Indian sepoys – were added three buffaloes, six camels, four donkeys and two mules. All the animals would die on the journey, the camels flogged to death by callous sepoys.

Livingstone hoped to reach Lake Bangweulu, trace the river northeast into Lake Tanganyika, then proceed triumphantly to Lake Albert and up the Nile, a terrifyingly difficult route. The tramp to Lake Nyasa (Lake Malawi) was appalling. The party hacked through jungle, crossed range after range of mountains, and failed to secure a dhow to cross the lake.

They were forced to round the southern end of the lake and proceed through countryside decimated by slaving and drought. Corpses lined the way. Their food supplies dwindled, the sepoys deserted, and by the time Livingstone reached the southern edge of Lake Tanganyika he had suffered malaria and dysentery and was 'a ruckle of bones'. His party was down to 11 men, dangerously small in a troubled land (Burton never travelled with under 130 porters).

One of the bearers fell and dropped the precious chronometers, throwing out his longitudinal reading, and for the next 18 months all his sightings were in error 20 miles eastward. This would eventually cost him his life. To add to this disaster, the porter carrying the medicine chest deserted with his load. Without quinine, Livingstone became so ill that his devoted servants, Chumah and Susi, built a hut for him and hung a blanket across the door so the other porters would not see him delirious. He was at the door of madness, and, in many decisions in the months which followed, it seems to have retained its hold.

Livingstone was saved by a well-supplied Arab slaving caravan, led by the infamous slaver Tippu Tip – a supreme irony, given his hatred of slavery. But he was treated kindly and recovered in Tip's care. Livingstone's supplies were dangerously low and he was now down to nine porters. The caravan was heading for Ujiji but Livingstone decided to push south to Lake Bangweulu. On hearing this, five more of his followers deserted.

The rains had begun and the party were often up to their waists in water for hours. Livingstone located a large river named Lualaba. The source of the Nile at last! But he was wrong: it was the source of the Congo River. He would never know. On the way back he contracted pneumonia and became delirious, seeing faces staring at him from every bit of wood.

He was saved again by an Arab caravan. Its leader, Bogharib, made a litter for him, had him carried and nursed him back to health. In Ujiji Livingstone hoped to find supplies sent up to him from Zanzibar by the governor, John Kirk, as a result of a letter he had dispatched with Tippu Tip. He arrived to discover the supplies had been pilfered.

::

Livingstone wrote 40 letters while in Ujiji, but only one of them reached the coast: the one asking Kirk for more supplies. While waiting for these he joined Bogharib on a journey west to Bambarre on the Lualaba where he hoped to trace the river northwards.

Passing through an area named Manyuema he discovered many of the tribes were cannibals – one of his porters, James, was killed and eaten. At Bambarre he was too sick to follow the river and spent seven months convalescing in the village. His writing during this time was tinged with madness. Following speculations of the writer Herodotus (who wrote in the fifth century BC), he now decided the Nile rose from between two hills with conical tops. Two Arabs Livingstone questioned said they had seen the hills west of Lake Bangweulu. They became the missionary's goal.

At a village on the Lualaba, Nyangwe, Livingstone witnessed a horrific slaughter when Arabs opened fire on Africans in the market place after an argument over prices. Around 500 people were shot as they ran. The missionary was outraged, and left the caravan vowing never to travel with Arabs again. When he returned to Ujiji he discovered with a sinking heart that his new supplies had again been looted. He was in a desperate position.

While deciding what to do, he heard that a white man had recently left Tabora with a huge caravan. Three months later, on 28 October 1871, Susi dashed up to Livingstone shouting 'An Englishman is coming!' A few minutes later the journalist Henry Morton Stanley, beside a bearer holding the American flag, walked up to Livingstone, stuck out his hand and uttered the memorable words: 'Dr Livingstone, I presume?'

::

Despite Livingstone's dislike of Europeans in Africa, the two men got on famously. Stanley, a much younger man, regarded Livingstone as something of a saint, all the while realising that in finding him after the missionary had been 'lost' for six years, his own career was assured. He was awed by his own sense of occasion.

Livingstone, for his part, couldn't believe that Stanley or his employer, James Gordon Bennett, who owned the *New York Herald*, should consider Livingstone worthy of such an expensive expedition.

Stanley was indeed head of one of the most expansively supplied expeditions of the century. No expense had been spared. Good food and the best medicines available restored the missionary's health in remarkably short time. The two set off for the north of Lake Tanganyika to see if the Nile flowed out of it (they found a stream flowing into the lake, which killed that theory).

By November 1871 Stanley knew he had to leave: he had a story to tell. It would sweep all other news off the front pages across the world. He would canonise Livingstone, a man 'as near an angel as the nature of living man will allow'. Perhaps more importantly, the account Livingstone wrote about the massacre of villagers at Nyangwe and published in the *New York Herald* was used by the abolitionist lobby to force the hand of the British government, which banned the sale of all slaves worldwide, blockaded Zanzibar until the sultan acceded to that order, and closed the slave market in Stone Town forever. Livingstone did not live to hear about it.

The missionary accompanied Stanley to Tabora, where the two men parted. Livingstone waited there for five months for the men and supplies Stanley had promised. When they arrived he set off for Lake Bangweulu in search of the two hills and four fountains.

Instead of guiding him round the lake, his faulty chronometers, aided by stormy conditions, led him deeper into the swamps around its shore. Racked with malaria, dysentery and severe anal bleeding, he died kneeling beside his bed in a rough grass hut.

Chumah and Susi decided to take his body to the coast. They buried his entrails, dried out his body, wrapped it in cloth, bark and tar. Then the party carried it more than 3000 kilometres through dangerous country to Bagamoyo and laid it outside the church of the Holy Ghost Fathers.

From the coast it was transported to Zanzibar, then to Southampton. As the steamer bearing the coffin appeared, the Royal Horse Artillery fired a 21-gun salute. The body was conveyed to London by special train and the burial took place in Westminster Abbey.

All Livingstone's faults and errors seemed forgotten. 'Westminster Abbey has opened its doors to men who have played larger and greater parts in the history of mankind,' wrote one newspaper editor. 'But seldom has been admitted one more worthy – one more unselfish in his devotion to duty – one whose ruling desire was stronger to benefit his kind and advance the sum of human knowledge and civilization – than this brave, modest, self-sacrificing, African explorer.' It was a fitting tribute.

::

So what can be said of this strange adventure in pursuit of an odd man long dead? One thing for sure, he's cast a long shadow. In towns and cities where colonial names have been changed to suit local politics there is always a Livingstone road or square.

Everyone who enquired about the nature of our quest (except the hotelier in Carnarvon) recognised his name, had learned of him in school and wished us well on our way. His name, it seems, is associated with that which is good about European contact with Africa. He is seen as the man who ended slavery.

But there remains a vexing question: why did Livingstone literally kill himself in pursuit of so bizarre a quest as the source of a river? It is likely that he suffered from an overwhelming sense of failure: a missionary who made but one convert; a husband and father who had failed; an explorer who had misled the British government by his miscalculations; a campaigner whose plan to settle missionaries up the Shire River had led to failure and the death of a bishop. The British government had snubbed him, offering him (in his estimation) a pittance with no pension. In his footsteps slavers followed.

He had never understood the adulation of the British public. But when he lost it he felt the sting keenly.

Finding the source of the Nile would be his redemption, the jewel he could carry back home with pride. In that, too, he failed. He would never know how he would later be revered, or of his part in the abolition of slavery.

Livingstone had once written that when he died, he would like it to be in some far-flung, forgotten corner of Africa. In that he certainly succeeded.

As we zigzagged up his meandering trail we found much of the Africa he travelled desperately poor and, in some places, at war. Much of the wilderness at which he marvelled is despoiled and overpopulated.

Yet the fact that we travelled where we did, were welcomed as we were and met so many fine people of disparate cultures – and did so in relative safety – is a tribute to his dream for Africa. The continent in which he adventured is, without a doubt, still a wonderful place to explore.

We travelled to honour him, and his trail did not disappoint us.

WAYWARD
EXPEDITIONS

The desert road north

There were two possible outcomes to the final push to Cairo. One would have us rolling past the pyramids and Sphinx into the great city, cracking a beer (if we could find one during Ramadan) and declaring: 'We did it!'

The other would be to buy a photograph of the pyramids, drop a picture of the Land-Rover into it by crafty computer manipulation, then run a headline on the front cover declaring: 'We did it!' Because the Landy would be either upside down in a sand dune or forever grounded by an oaf with a uniform and gun somewhere between Khartoum and Luxor.

While the security police stripped our vehicle in Wadi Halfa, or as we waved it goodbye – impounded – in Aswan, the second conclusion seemed more likely.

But I digress ....

::

I flew into Addis Ababa to join Mike Copeland for the final leg of the Cape-to-Cairo odyssey, feeling anxious about travelling through Sudan, a state that has turned civil war into a way of life. Three other colleagues had travelled in relays from Cape Town to Addis, and my part was the final leg. Mike, the stalwart, was going the whole way and my job was to keep him company with a notebook and a camera.

Ethiopia is a wonderful country full of surprises and gentle people, but Addis has little to recommend it: we left the Rasta city early. The air was already a nose-searing brown. Mike has an umbilical attachment to the place, but to me it's a pile of villas, shops, factories and high-rises with their heads in smog and their feet in slime. It was good to be moving out.

Then, of course, there was the matter of Ethiopian roads. One soon realises they were constructed for children, people on foot, donkeys, cows, goats, sheep and dogs. Motorised vehicles come as a complete surprise – even though the first 100 kilometres north of Addis is fast, blacktop highway. If you look at a map of Ethiopia you'll understand why. Considering its size, there are remarkably few roads. One gets the impression that roads are unusual, recent things that cut across ancient peopleways.

We soon lost the tar and bounded along on what was probably the undermatter of an old Italian-built road, the top surface long gone. This took us down into a vast gorge at the bottom of which slithered the Nile, then through the village of Debre Markos (good for sandwiches and tea) and on to endless-seeming diversions which wove round road construction.

Twelve hours and around 500 kilometres after leaving Addis – and in the dangerous dark – we swirled dustily into Bahir Dar and the welcome arms of the Papyrus Hotel. That night we slept within maybe 300 metres of the source of the Blue Nile.

::

We left Bahir Dar under a softly rising sun and wound our way along a passable road to just outside Gondar. At a ragged village named Azezo we filled up with diesel and began the descent to the Sudanese border. We anticipated the usual road from hell.

What a surprise! It had been completely rebuilt and, somewhere beyond Aykel, it tipped us off the Ethiopian escarpment towards the lowlands of Sudan. We dropped from 2300 metres to around 750 through spectacular mountain passes studded with weird, domed inselbergs. This is the escarpment that threw back Napoleon's expeditionary forces, Mohammed Ali's Egyptian invaders, the mad Mamelukes, the Turkish Beys, General Gordon's mixed bag of colonisers and even the intrepid Samuel Baker and the beautiful slave who became his wife. Looking back we understood why. Behind us rose a wall of mountains sliced by deep canyons and roaring rivers.

As we descended, the temperature rose. Out on the plain we were in another place entirely. Savanna replaced mountain cedars, and neat villages of square houses were replaced by round grass huts. We could have been in Tanzania, Kenya or Mozambique. The border was chaotic, so we backtracked to Shedi and the Sak Besak Hotel, where we settled back amid the hum of village life. Supper was ordered over a Bedele beer – *tibs* (meat pieces) for Mike and a vegetable omelette for me. The rooms had double beds with mosquito nets. Honestly, who could complain?

::

We bumped our way to the busy town of Gedaref – where we tried to get travel permits, but the security police shooed us out – then found a fine tarmac road to Wad Medani. The civil war in Sudan has been going on for 40-odd years and in that time more than two million people have been killed. But it's hard to believe, because the Sudanese are the friendliest, warmest, most sharing people I've ever met.

As it was Ramadan, everyone ate 'breakfast' as the sun set, and we were simply included in the process. In the villages and towns we were never allowed to pay for a meal. And what delicious food – tomato, onion and feta salad, bean and cheese dip, falafels, maize dough with lamb sauce, fruit juice and Pepsi.

First stop was the Nile Hotel on the banks of the river in Wad Medani. As the sun sank and the muezzin called, a mat was rolled out on the hotel veranda. We took off our shoes, sat cross-legged round bowls and dipped in, using freshly baked bread as a scoop. A coal-black Dinka schoolboy (the Dinkas are from the south) was hauled in to translate for us.

'Where are you from?'

'South Africa.'

'Where is that?'

As was to be customary with almost everyone we spoke to after that, I hauled out the map and pointed.

'Aah, so you are Africans too?'

Next day as we were rolled through a flat, endless plain, we saw a dark line crossing the road. Through the heat shimmer it resolved itself into a camel caravan. Sword-armed, cloaked men on huge beasts were shepherding strange-looking, long-tailed sheep and dozens of camels. On some camels were colourful canopies – small tents really – probably for women and young children.

It was a scene virtually unchanged in thousands of years. We stopped and watched, mesmerised, as the caravan swung out across the scrub desert until it was swallowed by mirage. A bit further on we came upon a very modern affair. The Sudanese seem to have no restriction on how many people can ride a lorry. They hang on to the sides, sit on top of bales, perch cross-legged on the cab roof. The things look like giant hedgehogs. And they're completely unstable. One had toppled over in the road, killing four passengers. After that we gave the hedgehog trucks a wide berth. Finally we made it to Khartoum.

::

Travelling is a strange business. To have been in Khartoum is somehow more poignant than *being* in Khartoum. Being there involves dust, dirt, discomfort, noise, suspect food, dicey water and being homesick. Having been there is amazing. Memory, learning and mind weave together a cloth more fabulous than the indifferent roar of its traffic.

This town has been the goal of adventurers like Burton, Baker and Emin Pasha who sought the source of the Nile, and men like Napoleon, Mohammed Ali, General Gordon and Lord Kitchener who wished to capture and control Nilotic Africa.

To Khartoum the Egyptians and Turks dragged millions of Dinka and Nubian slaves, reducing the population of Sudan by catastrophic numbers. There Gordon stood on the balcony of his fort, watching the besieging troops of the Mahdi break through his Egyptian defences and hack their way through the streets towards him. There his decapitated head was paraded on a pole and used as a football.

An outraged Britain sent Lord Kitchener to avenge his death. He blasted his way upriver by gunboat, took Khartoum, desecrated the Mahdi's grave and paraded his skull. The British public were revolted.

As we were camping at the Khartoum Yacht Club (next to the now-beached gunboat) a cat peed on the tent near my head. The toilet had not been flushed, and stank. But next morning the black-shouldered kites were patrolling the river – they fly so deftly – and wagtails were hopping on the lawn. Most of Khartoum was sleeping off the excesses of the previous night's Ramadan celebrations and the air was cool.

::

At Khartoum the Nile curves eastwards, but we took a good tar road north through the desert to meet it as it curved west again. There is no road from Abu Dom, where we rejoined the Nile, to Dongola, or from there to Wadi Halfa 600 kilometres further north. There are just vague tracks and a tree line along the Nile. To the west, peach desert sand to the horizon.

The Nile is brave to have chosen this route to the sea. We put JJ Cale on the CD player and tunnelled through the wasteland, billowing dust and music out behind. It was wonderfully incongruous. That evening we got as far as El Goled Bahri where we set up camp among some palm trees and watched the moon rise over the Nile.

Next morning, after much hit-and-miss tracking through the sand, we made the old Nubian capital of Dongola. It is a delightful town of ancient trees, squat houses and a busy souk selling almost everything. There we crossed the Nile by ferry and headed up the east bank. The villages were the most beautiful we'd seen – neat, painted and with deep trees and cool verandas. We ended up looping right back south at one point, which caused us some concern, but then we discovered it was the only way round some wild, black granite

mountains. Along the way we stopped to see the Third Cataract. The rocks round there – granite or sedimentary – were burned as black as the Nubian people.

We stopped in the small village of Majaziep in the Abu Sara region of Nubia on the Nile. After a day of hectic, roadless driving over sand and desert pavement the village appeared when we badly needed it. The locals looked at us as though we'd dropped in from space. But, as usual, the children broke the ice and they soon surrounded me. We were asked to break our fast with the village, then put up our tents and slept to the sound of wind in the palms and lapping river.

∷

If anyone wants to do the sort of wild 4x4 travel they can boast about over a beer years later, they should try the run from Abu Dom to Wadi Halfa. It's so off the map nobody round there knows what a map is. With ancient tombs, abandoned mud forts, camel caravans, no roads and hooded people, it's about as exotic as it gets.

Wadi Halfa, however, was another matter. If you think you understand bureaucracy and have not been to Wadi Halfa, you are an infant in this arcane science. It began in Abri where we asked the wrong man where to buy tomatoes: he turned out to be 'security' and pulled us in. Passports? Travel documents? We had tried twice to get travel documents from security offices in Sudan but they had merely copied our passport details and sent us packing.

Worse was to follow. When we entered Sudan at Gallabat, despite an hour of poring over our documents and making stamping noises, it seems they had failed to stamp our passports. In Sudan, we were to find out, customs and passport control are never at the same place, and there are no signs to show you where they are. And anyway, we don't read Arabic.

So at Abri, after an hour of discussion, a security cop with a cheap black briefcase was settled in our back seat and rode with us for half a day to Wadi Halfa – with our offending passports in his pocket.

When we stopped for lunch under the only tree in 50 kilometres, he flung open the briefcase, whipped out a mean-looking Uzi sub-machine pistol and leapt out the Landy. Was this to be our execution point?

No, it was for snakes, he said, and prowled the tree. If there had been one it would have been blasted straight into the arms of Allah.

Next day, in Wadi Halfa, the security police went over our possessions with all the aggressive thoroughness of adolescents with power. They even had the good-cop-bad-cop routine and the 'maybe you will never leave Sudan' solo. The conversation went something like this:

'What's this?'

'Radio.'

'What?'

'BBC.'

'Oh. This?'

'Fridge.'

'Open it!'

'And this?'

'Rooftop tent.'

'What?'

'Camping.'

'Oh. This?'

'Cameras.'

I opened the bag. It looked worryingly formidable: a long, black 200 mm lens, two cameras, a flash, several other lenses and my round film-storage tin, which looks like a Claymore mine. The flash seemed to interest the bad cop with the shades. I switched it on and flashed it. He felt the warmth of the bulb for a while, thoughtfully.

Eventually, after two hours of this, they eased up. They then took a couple of hours to write two letters of the 'name, occupation, address, reason for being in Sudan' sort. I swear: two hours. With these letters duly sealed in a brown envelope, a security cop accompanied us to passport control.

More letters were written, slowly. We were given forms to fill in. One was an entrance to Sudan (we were at our port of departure), the other permission to travel through Sudan (we were on our way out). All that cost about US$30.

Then we needed *departure* stamps. Also two photocopies each of passports, visas and customs forms. The photocopier was at the telegraph office. When we got there the power was off. So we waited … and waited. There was a pair of crutches in the corner. Eventually we got our photocopies. The next stamp cost $4 and, oh yes, we had to buy the files in which to place our documents ($3). We refused the last item, point-blank. The captain will not look at forms not in a folder, we were told. We gave him a hard look. He did.

We left, eventually, with exit stamps and bleeding money. Next stop the customs. No, sorry, they were busy. Tomorrow. We went to buy ferry tickets to Aswan (US$650 for the Land-Rover and US$50 for us, plus US$300 a month to be in Egypt). But the ticket office was closed for the day.

We returned to a lean-to that passes for a café. There we met a traveller named Stephan, who was having similar problems getting out of the country. 'If God wanted to give Earth an enema,' he grumbled, 'he'd stick it right in Wadi Halfa!'

::

We eventually escaped Sudan, though we often thought it would be impossible. The Land-Rover was loaded onto a pontoon which was strapped to the side of a battered ferry. After a final round of customs and passport hassles and the payment of still more money, we set sail on a 27-hour trip up the High Aswan Dam to Aswan.

We docked, got the Landy off the pontoon, were shooed back on board, had our passports stamped, then waited. Three hours later nobody had embarked and tempers among the 300 or so passengers crushed into the passageways were rising.

Mike and I backed out of the crush, climbed onto the roof of the dock from an upper deck, shinned down a pole and regained our Landy. A fierce little sergeant shouted and huffed, but he had a crowd to hold back.

The customs man looked at our *carnet de passage*, established that the name on it belonged to the owner and not one of us, and refused to stamp it. He effectively impounded the vehicle. We would have to go to Cairo (1000 kilometres north), and get an endorsement from the Automobile Club of Egypt. To do this they would have to contact the AA in South Africa.

Beyond that he wouldn't budge. So we cadged a lift from the docks into town and took a train to Cairo. It was Friday (the Muslim sabbath) and the AA there wasn't open. On Saturday it was, but not in South Africa. And so it went.

It took us five days to clear the vehicle, and each day we had to pay the Aswan customs for 'protecting' it. The customs official, Mr Hammam, then asked us for a 'present' for helping us. We declined.

The total cost of getting the Landy into Egypt from Wadi Halfa – including the ferry (you may not go by any other means) came to a bit more than R10,000. After that, all I can say is that while we can tell you how to drive through Sudan and Egypt to Cairo, we do not recommend it.

We made Luxor as the sun was sinking, having been forced to travel in convoy by military types with wailing sirens (tourists were gunned down some time ago and the police were making sure it wouldn't happen again).

Now you may be irritated by the insatiable bureaucracy of Egypt, worn down by incessant tat-sellers shoving tourist trash in your face, infuriated by everyone showing you what you already know and demanding baksheesh for it; but when you stand in front of the temple of Karnak, stare down the half-kilometre avenue of sphinxes to the Temple of Luxor or gaze, dumbstruck, at the illuminated artwork in the tunnels of the Valley of Kings, you know why you've come to Egypt.

We booked into the Happy Land Hotel in an alley bedecked with the bunting of Eid. Our aerial did some damage to it on the way. Happy Land is something to behold. It is possibly the most spotless place in all Egypt and, believe me, that is a jewel, given the filth strewn about the place.

We did the tourist thing in Luxor, Karnak and the Valley of Kings amid thousands of others, busload upon busload of them. But the temples, palaces and tombs are so huge, so dramatic, so beautiful that tourists don't matter, somehow. They're just sidelined by the grandeur of it all. The next day we decided to give the convoys the slip and head out into the Western Desert.

::

I had been looking for a reason to like Egypt and I finally found it. We had to sneak out of Luxor, with its touts and police, take back roads and then, finally, the empty, rather scary roads into the boundless desert.

First there was endless gravel desert floor, then there were giant barchan dunes, then megalith molehills in the weirdest scenery imaginable (when we stopped the silence was utter). We drove for maybe 350 kilometres and came to the Dakhla oasis system.

By the time we reached the settlement of Mut, within the Dakhla system, all the hassles of Egypt had been redeemed. Surrounded by fields and newer constructions, its heart is an ancient, crumbling citadel which long pre-dates Roman times, some of it abandoned but much of it still very much alive. Its mudpacked buildings lean on one another, connect and turn lanes into cool tunnels. Mudslap walls billow and ripple in the slow winds of time. Smells of cooking and incense drift out of dark doorways, mingling with the sound of women singing and children playing.

In the square, the evening we arrived, old men – Nubians, Libyans, Berbers and Sudanese – sat watching a video of Robin Williams playing Patch Adams (subtitled in Arabic) with the alert, puzzled looks of desert fennec foxes at their first obedience class.

We sat at a table, ordered chai tea, refused the proffered hookah and settled down amid amicable company to watch the night deepen. Robin Williams was soon consigned to oblivion. Nobody hassled us, offered us anything we didn't want or demanded baksheesh. The old men merely glanced at us with their dark, sun-wrinkled eyes, assessed us, nodded and accepted us in the old desert tradition of Muad Dib. Strangers were guests and it was impolite to pry.

Next morning was the first day of Eid. Seemingly hundreds of muezzins sang, chanted, howled and, eventually, croaked the sun into the sky. It was a stirring performance.

Mut was waking to the end of the fast. It was party time....

That day, though, we had an appointment with the dead. Near the oasis of El Kasr is a Roman fort and a hill into which caves have been burrowed. Inside were dozens of Romans – maybe 2000 years old – lying side by side, small, shrivelled, clothed and with wisps of hair, all mummified by the dry, desert air. The old quarter of El Kasr is a treasure, continuously occupied since time immemorial and sprinkled with fine old Ottoman buildings.

From there we drove 290 kilometres through an almost featureless Sahara to Farafra, where we overnighted in some luxury at the El Badawiya Hotel. Next morning we left before sunrise. As the golden ball of dawn slipped up over the horizon, we dived off the road into the White Desert. It's a strange place, with tortured limestone formations – thousands upon thousands of them – encircled by yellow, shifting sands.

After that the desert flattened to dead featurelessness. We could have been in mid-ocean.

Cairo appeared at the edge of the nothing in the form of new high-rise apartments; incongruous, newly painted and empty. Gradually the road became busier, powerlines began snaking across our path and, eventually, we were in heavy, hooting city traffic.

We drove into Tahrir Square (Cairo's Piccadilly Circus), parked in a dirty back alley and booked into the Ismalia House Hotel. We'd made it!

Early next morning I awoke, feeling flat. So we were in Cairo, Mother of the World, city of 16 million people. There seemed to be one final thing we needed to do. We dressed, powered up the Landy and headed out of town to pay our respects to the Sphinx. Near Giza we could see the tops of the pyramids, but they disappeared behind buildings until we drove round a cluster of tea shops. There they suddenly were. They stopped us in our tracks.

What stood before us has been so iconised, stylised and embedded in images of popular culture that there had been a strong possibility that the real thing would never measure up to its popular image.

The Sphinx and its pyramids, so glorious and huge, did the opposite. They trashed all representations of themselves in the sheer, outrageous exhibitionism of their startling construction.

After that we went back to the hotel for breakfast. As far as I was concerned, we had finally arrived. The trip was complete: we had succeeded in our quest. Would I do it again? Not on your life!

Time travelling on the Lake of Stars

There were five cows in the lifeboats. They hadn't been there the previous evening so they must have been loaded from some lakeside village during the night. Probably Metangula. They didn't look happy swinging there, brown eyes wide with terror and noses wet from spit and thrashing about.

Later that morning the two boats were lowered off Cóbué, cows and all. On the bow of each boat was stencilled MAXIMUM LOAD – 22 PERSONS, so maybe it was considered okay to pack 11 goats, several hundred chickens, a puppy and a flapping duck plus 11 bags of maize, two beds and a heap of people on top of the cows, which by then seemed to have swooned into a state of torpor.

Heaven knows how all that was landed on the beach, with no jetty and a nasty little chop on the lake. All I can say is that the lifeboat crew of the *Ilala* – Lake Malawi's floating peasant bus – are consummate boatmen. They yell a lot, and sometimes throw both goods and people ashore or onto the ship, but you never get a sense they're out of control. Their boats, like the *Ilala*, are dented and scratched, but their motors always seem to start and they do wonderful things with ropes and hooks.

I'd boarded the *Ilala* – an ancient, interestingly bashed but undoubtedly enduring lake steamer – at Monkey Bay, down south, and had bagged a cabin with an en suite bathroom and an armchair – by *Ilala* standards, pure luxury. The lower deck was dense with peasant farmers and small-time traders with their rolls, bags, children, goats, ducks, chickens and – as I discovered at Cóbué – even cattle. For many lake-shore Malawians, the ship is just about their only link to the outside world – a slightly tatty white angel which appears out of the lake with unfailing regularity and seems to have no restriction on whom or what it is prepared to ferry between heaven and hell.

By all accounts, the peasants were starving just then – some eating green maize, others winnowing grass. It seems some government official had sold Malawi's maize reserves to another country. There were rumours he had also pocketed the money and that he had then been promoted. About 65 per cent of Malawi's 11 million people live below the poverty line. The busy trans-lake micro-commerce between Malawi and Mozambique was probably keeping a good many alive.

The names of the southern lake villages upon which the *Ilala* bestows its blessings roll off your tongue like quicksilver: Chilinda, Chipoka, Makanjira, Nkhotakota, Metangula, Likoma. Each had its huts, its canoes and its crowds.

Likoma Island, however, also had its cathedral, a building as out of place as a whale in a fish tank. Likoma is a few kilometres off the Mozambican shore and is only eight kilometres long. Oddly, though, it was the headquarters of the Anglican Church of Malawi until the 1940s. The reason had to do with Bishop Chauncy Maples who, with his friend the Reverend William Johnson, established a mission there in 1886 as a project of the Universities Mission to Central Africa – inspired by David Livingstone. Maples was drowned in Nkhotakota Bay on the way to his bishopric.

In 1903 work began on the huge cathedral, which was dedicated to St Peter. It's an extraordinary building for such a remote place – 100 metres long, 25 wide, with stained-glass windows and elaborate stalls. It was built on the spot where Maples witnessed suspected witches being burned alive. The crucifix above the altar is one of the few made from the wood of a tree beside which Livingstone's heart was buried in Zambia.

At Nkhata Bay we gained more steerage passengers and lost most of the deck and cabin passengers. I was rather sorry about that. The deck passengers were almost as colourful as those down below; travellers who pitched their tents on deck or curled up on the hard benches to brave out the night in the open.

There was a Belgian couple, Derek and Meika – nutbrown with legs all scratched – who had been cycling the backroads of southern Malawi and were hitching a ride to explore more backroads up north.

Big Ben was an Aussie who ran a guesthouse in Cóbué, owned a bit of wild beach and was an expert on the commercial and social benefits of marijuana. Little Ben was from London. He'd met Big Ben, abandoned plans for a world trip, bought an expensive video camera and was making a digital diary of his life in Mozambique, plus helping around the guesthouse. The trouble was that, not long after Little Ben arrived, Big Ben decided he needed to head back to civilisation. Little Ben looked a bit crestfallen.

Patrick ran a lodge and some community projects in Mozambique. He'd once cycled from Addis Ababa to Johannesburg, which took five months. Jan was a Hollander who'd driven from Amsterdam to Cape Town via Morocco, West Africa, Chad and Sudan – not the easiest route.

North of Nkhata Bay you really feel you're in the Great Rift Valley. The lake is 585 kilometres long and 80 at its widest point, and while the shoreline of the southern half is rather flat, north of Nkhata the Kandoli Mountains rise up aggressively, backed by the Nyika and Viphya plateaus. This is high miombo-woodland country with villages wedged between steep slopes and the water's edge.

When we dropped anchor off Usisya, the scene was so saturated with metaphor and historical allusion it was difficult to believe it was real – and that we were in the 21st century. If it were a movie shoot, the clapperboard would read: 'First Arrival on Wild, Foreign Shore'.

David Livingstone had witnessed such a reception on the Lower Zambezi from the deck of *Ma-Robert*, and Captain James Cook from the bridge of *Endeavour* as he made landfall in Tahiti. Albert Schweitzer described with delight the welcome given on arriving at Lambaréné up the Ogooué River, where he would build a hospital and capture the imagination of Europe, and Joseph Conrad imbued a similar scene with savage menace in *Heart of Darkness*.

As the ship dropped anchor, hundreds of villagers flooded out of grass huts and lined the shore in a colourful, babbling throng. Dugout canoes were dragged into the water and arrowed towards us, their paddlers whooping. On the shore the crowd heaved and billowed like a single living thing.

Behind the human crush edging the beach, huge baobab and mango trees dwarfed rough grass huts. Beyond them thick forest cloaked the slopes of muscular mountains, dipping into valleys beneath snakes of morning mist and reappearing on distant, storm-topped peaks.

I gawped at the scene for a while, then hitched a ride on one of the lifeboats to see what Archangel *Ilala* looked like from the shore. As I jumped into the surf, a wave whacked me ashore into the arms of a yelling hubbub of mostly naked children, who took up a ringing chant: 'Photo, photo ....' Which of course made photography impossible.

The *Ilala* certainly looked magnificent, huge against the foreground of crude huts, and startlingly white in a world of blues and greens. I dodged my young followers long enough to discover a backpacker place named Usisya Beach Lodge – basic grass huts, hammocks and heaven.

The lakeshore had a smell all of its own. It was drenched with the heavy linden-sweetness of flowering trees, compounded with the fusty, antique odours of bats, wood smoke and wet earth. It pulsated with a strange rhythm. The throbbing sounds of countless human voices rose and fell in time to the everlasting beat of drums and the thud of pestles pounding maize in wooden mortars, while to this was added the incessant contrapuntal zing of amatory cicadas.

The effect was trance-inducing. Joseph Conrad had described such an experience as 'being captured by the incredible, which is of the very essence of dreams'.

The ship's hooter sounded, shaking me out of my reverie, and I scampered back into the waiting lifeboat. To be stranded there, it occurred to me as the boat pulled away, would not be a great hardship.

North of Usisya everything goes under the heading Spectacular. Subtitles run to Awesome, Exotic and Romantic. It was the rainy season and as we weighed anchor at Nkhata Bay a storm slammed into the rising sun. A straight line of pinkish cloud appeared across the horizon about 1000 metres above the lake. Below it, streaks of rain were rippling like the legs of a millipede; above rose a massive thunderhead, stacked in layers of variegated grey to its bulbous anvil haloed in golden light. We sailed straight at the storm but, before we reached it, shafts of sunlight seemed to have blasted it to death, leaving a few tattered memories of the dawn performance.

Those who sail Lake Malawi know it to be a singularly alien and exotic thing, elemental and undisciplined, a sleeping giant liable at any moment to rage with aboriginal fury. From the decks of the *Ilala* the thrusting landscape of Eocene catastrophe trembled through the heat haze, reminding us of the red-hot world that had fashioned the rift.

Ungovernable storms are known to sweep suddenly from a clear sky across the waters of the lake, and when certain clouds descend, battalions of dervish-dancing waterspouts leap hundreds of metres into the air to meet them, as though trying to escape some lake demon below.

As we puttered towards Ruarwe and Tcharo, clouds of lake flies in their nuptial flight seemed intent on emulating the waterspouts, looking exactly like the smoke from some hull-down steamer.

This is a lake of moods, sometimes spilling its banks for no apparent reason; at other times retreating, stranding boats and jetties. There is no tide to mix its deep waters, and at times the lighter oxygenated surface water skids to and fro across the useless, stagnant layer below, as though the lake was being rocked like a gargantuan bathtub.

We turned at Chilumba, just north of Mount Waller, and headed back towards Monkey Bay. As it was the rainy season, the lake was shy with its colours, but near Likoma Island the clouds rolled back for the grand evening performance for which Malawi is justly famous.

As the sun sank westwards the waters became an enchanted mirror, tilted to reflect the languid artistry of a painted sky. In the strange silence of the dying day the waters glowed deep crimson, then almost reluctantly changed to silken, cyclamen purple as they waited for the evening breeze to caress their magic texture and set lines of amber ripples swimming slowly towards the farther shore. This signalled all the colours on the water to fade like courtiers from an audience chamber, until at last only an imperial presence of molten gold remained.

The loveliness of the mountains was scarcely less compelling. Theirs were pastel shades: pale lavender melting imperceptibly on one side into pearly grey and on the other into a luminous Madonna blue.

Suddenly it was night. A layer of moon-silver spread over the mountains and the sky trembled with the myriad stars of Africa. The placid water reflected each shining point of light, and as I turned to go below, it seemed we were moving through a watery universe, divorced from space and time. It was a sublime farewell.

Next morning the lifeboats were full of goats.

Tracking the Tropic of Capricorn

Emmanuel Petrakakis, when we met him in Maputo, was about to give a lecture in Johannesburg on the importance of colonising Mars. He is, you must understand, a postmodern man, something of a specialist on anti-globalisation, space travel, Art Deco and the legendary LM (Lourenço Marques) prawn, which his father virtually invented.

Over a huge clam chowder, red wine and, yes, delicious LM prawns, Emmanuel's Socratic mind explored the rise and fall of civilisations, Mars, the architecture of Pancho Guedes and how his father paid his way over from Greece in 1938 by playing a lyre aboard ship.

Papa Petrakakis started a tea pavilion where the Costa do Sol Restaurant now stands, serving crumbed prawns to hunters who ventured out of town to shoot guinea fowl. Holidaying South Africans – who wouldn't think of eating a prawn in those days – scoffed the little crumbed tasties by the bucketload, and only later found out what they were. Thus, according to Emmanuel, the LM prawn was born.

There was another subject which required discussion that evening: the way west. Before the night was out we'd spattered our Michelin map with peri-peri sauce, and accidentally dipped a corner in red wine, but had also planned a route clear across Southern Africa to

Swakopmund. Two weeks to drive from the Indian to the Atlantic Ocean through four countries. Our route would cross from subtropical Mozambique to the moonscapes of the Namib Desert by way of the Lowveld, the Highveld, the Bushveld and the Kalahari. Let's just say it seemed like a good idea at the time.

First, though, Maputo needed exploring. It's a city that wears the scars of colonialism, war, arid Marxism, boom and neglect on almost every street except Friedrich Engels Avenue, on which, ironically, can be found the United States embassy.

There's an ancient, battle-scarred fort, built by the Portuguese in the 17th century, trashed by the Dutch, built again, trashed by the British and built yet again. It's now a museum with green lawns, guns and a marble statue of some Portuguese commander, his nose broken, standing forlornly in a corner like a punished child.

Graceful though neglected colonial buildings rub shoulders with equally neglected but still grand Art Deco fantasies. No-expense-spared, sea-facing palaces of the rich jostle with an extraordinary number of incomplete mansions which seem to have fallen foul of changing political or economic fortunes.

The roads have potholes, the pavements are often broken and the refuse department has long ago lost control of rubbish collection. But the place has vibrancy, a busy bustle that's infectious. People of all shades and classes mill and mix happily, though some drive well-polished 4x4s and others hobble on war-issue crutches. It's a city aptly described as the Havana of Africa – poverty with a beat.

Friedrich Engels Avenue, though, is a road of embassies, high walls, guards and a fine restaurant – Villa Italia, up on a ridge and a world apart. Not far away are the grand hotels, the Polana with its old elegance and the Holiday Inn, which owns a piece of pristine beach-front. At their feet fishermen in dugouts trawl nets or cast into the shallow bay.

Our first night in Maputo was in the atmospheric, buzzy Costa do Sol; our last was in the somewhat austere luxury of the Holiday Inn, which shook to the reverberations of a spectacular, flashy storm. It was a good send-off for the trip towards the deserts of Namibia.

We whizzed through the two border posts with such ease it was almost disorienting. Customs and immigration officials smiled, stamped and waved us on. Having geared ourselves for the usual African passport ordeal, we felt like being let off school detention. Maybe they were impressed by the obvious pedigree of our no-nonsense-looking Colt – a highly kitted old friend from our earlier trip up Africa in the footsteps of David Livingstone.

Where would we spend the first night in South Africa? We consulted that most bountiful of sources, the Destinations pages of *Getaway*, and found what we needed. Near Kruger Park's Malelane Gate, just off the N4, is Thanda-Nani, a private game reserve. On first investigation it seemed to be simply an elegant bush lodge with the usual thatch and animals until, topping a rise, we were in Jurassic Park.

All round us were about 30 prehistoric beasts, snorting and jousting, some with armour-plated youngsters who challenged wildebeests and warthogs. Rhinos aren't exactly prehistoric, but they're about as far in that direction as mammals can get.

Thanda-Nani, it turned out, is both a reserve and a breeding ranch for rhinos and buffaloes – we'd driven into a rhino feeding station. It's owned by wildlife enthusiast John Hume and the lodge is run by Janine and Mark Nunns. We ate like piglets, slept in luxury and headed on west the next day.

Beyond Nelspruit the spectacular limestone caverns of Sudwala beckoned. They're really weird and wonderful, but our guide was uninformative and gallingly patronising. Someone should turn him into a stalagmite.

Soon afterwards the road began to rise on the broad shoulders of the Highveld. The valleys were softened by what seemed to be mist, but turned out to be pollution billowing out of a Sappi paper mill. With steam and smoke rising from its gloomy buildings and smoke stacks, it had all the attractions of William Blake's dark, satanic mills.

Bergwaters Lodge, up a green valley near Waterval Onder, appeared just when we needed it. It's owned by Max and Maralyn Wetschnig, who bought it five years ago as a run-down place of little interest to travellers. Now it has 13 rooms and a honeymoon suite complete with His and Her lion pictures above the bed and a bathroom graced with cavorting nymphs. Max trained as a chef in Vienna and has worked at top hotels round the world. Now he does Austrian-meets-Bushveld cooking and their guests return – again and again.

This is Jock of the Bushveld country and one can almost hear the yap of Sir Percy FitzPatrick's famous Staffy in the wooded kloofs. Some of the lesser known facts about Sir Percy are that he started life as a bank clerk, was arrested after the infamous Jameson Raid into the Transvaal and had a passion for irrigation. But Jock is how he's best remembered.

Up the Escarpment past Waterval Boven and we were on the Highveld. The air was brown with smoke from huge, coal-burning power stations. Why do people there – especially the maize farmers – put up with all that aerial muck?

The suffering sky stayed with us all the way to Pretoria, and lifted only as we wound our way past Krugersdorp and into the arms of the Magaliesberg. These are ancient bergs – a hundred times older than Mount Everest – and they feel it. Their origins were spectacular. Some 2000 million years ago, an immense upwelling of liquid rock – around 65,000 square kilometres of it and the largest known intrusion on earth – insinuated itself into the sedimentary bedding plains of the Highveld, undermining and weakening them.

Then, gradually, the mass subsided, dragging the centre downwards. Slabs of rock thousands of metres thick tilted into the morass of magma, and the broken edges rose up like the prows of sinking ships, forming jagged mountains all round the huge basin.

The Magaliesberg is the remains of part of this rim, now covered in woodland scrub and

dry forest, with Transvaal milk plum and wild elder woods beneath jagged cliffs. Here leopards, brown hyenas, jackals and caracals still prowl.

It was also the testing ground for proto-humans – in the nearby Sterkfontein Caves three-million-year-old remains of *Australopithecus africanus* have been dug up.

We plotted our way to Celtis Lodge, where Margot Barnett and her son, Mike, have somehow tapped into the ancient rhythms of the mountains. Celtis is quite consciously magic, with a stone labyrinth centred on a crystal, a tiny chapel which seats only six and the sound of nothing but the rustle of leaves in the breeze.

We ate, in romantic isolation, to the soft music of Crystal Healing and were served by a butler, Glynwell Chirwa – a perfect Nestor straight out of Tintin's Marlinspike Manor.

The thatched cottages, the unhurried atmosphere, the wide views and the gentle lowing of Mike's cows next morning made it a hard place to leave.

The sky was pale blue and pollution-free above rolling maize and sunflower fields between Koster and Swartruggens. We pulled into a garage and I asked the pump attendant what went on in Swartruggens. He thought for a while – for so long I expected some profundity – then shrugged and said: 'Nothing.'

The change in scenery along the N4, as you drop down into the Bushveld, is profound. Trees rose up to meet us, and rivers splashed happily down woody valleys. We were in Herman Charles Bosman country.

'There is no other place', the writer said of the Marico, 'that is so heavy with atmosphere, so strongly and darkly impregnated with the stuff of life that bears the authentic stamp of South Africa.'

Bosman taught at a school in the Marico for a mere six months in the 1920s, but in that time he gathered sufficient material to write 150 highly crafted Bushveld stories and achingly beautiful poetry. It was in Groot Marico that the unforgettable character of Oom Schalk Lourens and that deadly but delicious peach brandy were born.

If you're searching for the soul of the Marico, go by way of Egbert and Santa van Baart of The Art Factory. What they run is something between a craft shop, *koffiekamer* and travel service. Egbert, with impish blue eyes and a contemplative greying beard down his chest, is a near-perfect Oom Schalk reincarnation.

::

On advice – because of roadworks – we deviated northwards off the N4 just beyond Zeerust and crossed the border into Botswana at the tiny post of Ramotswa. You must have displeased some brass in the immigration service to be posted there.

It took only a few minutes to clear the paperwork and we were soon driving through the gates of Mokolodi Nature Reserve in search of a bed.

Mokolodi's an unusual place. It was established on 5000 hectares of donated land near Gaborone to promote wildlife conservation and provide environmental education for the people of Botswana. It's run by a private trust and includes a white-rhino breeding project, a cheetah transit station, a sanctuary for injured animals, an elephant programme (you can walk with them) and an education centre. It also has chalets, tented camps and an excellent restaurant.

That night we curled up under duvets in a tent. Apart from the occasional yip of a jackal, it was so quiet that the noisiest things were my thoughts.

From Mokolodi we rolled onto the Sir Seretse Khama Highway – more commonly known as the Trans-Kalahari Highway – and headed for distant Kang. Beyond a village named Kanye the hills (which once housed David Livingstone's mission station) disappeared, and we were soon on a road as flat as a table.

The Kalahari is surely one of the natural wonders of Africa. It's a sand mantle – the largest in the world – covering more than a million square kilometres and forming a shallow saucer across much of Botswana. Rainfall is erratic and what water falls is soon absorbed into the sand. Yet, despite the low rainfall, there were carpets of silver-tipped grass in seemingly endless woodlands for hundreds of kilometres.

The straight road can be mesmerising: there were two accidents and many skid marks – probably vehicles avoiding (or hitting) wandering animals.

In the middle of all this is Kang Ultra-Stop, a sleek new garage, shop, restaurant, pub and chalets. The road west from there was as straight as the road east, a line through a sun-baked confection of camel thorn, shepherd's trees and pale yellow grasses. It was like travelling through eternity, with the sky huge and the pale blue of a lilac-breasted roller's wing.

Some 260 kilometres of this later we nosed our way into Trail Blazers Camp near Ghanzi, a cluster of grass beehive huts in the middle of dry woodland. Soon some wild-looking San arrived, each wearing nothing but scraps of skin, and carrying a bow and arrows and wicked-looking spears.

Then began one of the most extraordinary experiences of the trip. We tracked through the bush as the hunter-gatherers foraged for food and herbs. These they found, on trees, in bushes and underground – so successfully it was clear they could feed a family with maybe an hour's foraging. Why bother to enter the modern age when you can do that? One hunter whizzed a stick in his hands for under a minute and had a fire blazing in which wild nuts were roasted.

That evening under a boma we were joined by Julian Butler, a local businessman who created Trail Blazers. Bushmen began trotting in from the dark. A fire was started and some young women gathered around it, clapping. More Bushmen appeared, and as the circle grew a few men started a shuffling dance. It soon became clear this wasn't a tourist performance but a serious trance dance.

One of the men suddenly doubled over clutching his stomach while his companions held him up and stroked his back. Then another went into trance, and another.

The older shaman eventually recovered and, his eyes unseeing, felt his way round the circle, holding several people, testing, according to Julian, for illnesses. I sat in the circle briefly and he grabbed my shoulders. It was like an electric shock down my spine.

We eventually traipsed off to bed in one of the huts. In the morning all that was left was a memory of wild, dancing figures in the firelight, the ashes of a fire and a furrowed circle where tiny feet had stamped to ancient rhythms.

::

The road from Ghanzi over the border into Namibia, through Gobabis and on to Windhoek, was the longest section of the trip – 540 kilometres with few features to relieve the eye. Not a place for agoraphobics. Windhoek, though, was worth the tedium. It's a delightful little city, wrapped round meandering hills. We celebrated our arrival in civilisation with a gourmet meal, then slept the sleep of travellers. In town next morning we got a parking ticket. Well, it's part of the price you pay for civilisation.

We headed north to Okahandja, then west. At Karibib the somewhat Mexican-feeling Western Restaurant was open for lunch, after which we hit the road again, chasing the sunset.

Quite suddenly, considering how flat it was, purple spikes appeared on the horizon: Spitzkoppe, Namibia's crystal mountains. Along the road was a double line of rough tables with thousands of different crystals being sold by desperately poor people, many of them children. Is it okay to hack the heart out of a crystal mountain and sell it at the roadside for a pittance? Looking at the sellers and the harsh environment, I guess it's their best option.

Gradually the trees reduced in size as our vehicle rumbled along. Then they vanished altogether, leaving only dollar bushes and boksdoorn in the wadis – and gravel to the horizon. Swakopmund announced its arrival with a long avenue of palms that led into a town which looked like the child of a relationship between Bremen and Hermanus. It's a really pretty town, with atmospheric old German colonial buildings and a vibrant pavement café culture.

We checked into a guest cottage, but our mission beckoned, so we dropped the bags and headed up the coast for a bit. At no particular place we turned onto the gravel plain and bounced towards the sea. On the beach gulls wheeled and there was that particularly kelpy west coast smell. There we sat watching the fat, orange sun dipping towards the sea as skeins of cormorants drew moving black lines across the sky.

Back in Maputo the waves of the Indian Ocean would be breaking across the road from Costa do Sol. LM prawns would be grilling. But we were 2704 kilometres away. Had Emmanuel got to Mars? Was there still smog over Mpumalanga? Had Margot Barnett found the path to enlightenment in the labyrinth? Was the Highveld still sinking into the magma? Right then, it didn't seem to matter.

The colours of Ethiopia

'I give you the colours of Ethiopia,' said Marishet Dires as his 14-year-old fingers deftly tied the cloth bracelet round my arm. 'No money, just friends, okay?'

'Okay, Marishet.'

We were on a bridge near Bahar Dar which spanned the powerful headwaters of the Blue Nile as it flowed from Lake Tana. He was returning from school ('two sessions, I'm afternoon') and wanted to practise his English.

I looked down at the amulet's finely-woven stripes of green, yellow and red – Rastafarian colours – and up at his shining white smile, delicate, honey-coloured features and rich black curls. His was a culture so ancient and sophisticated that when the people of Europe were building with mud and grass his ancestors were constructing stone palaces and carving elegant granite statues.

'What do the colours mean?' I asked.

'Green's for the land, yellow's for the church and red … red … I can't remember. Maybe you'll find out,' he grinned.

The colours of Ethiopia were rich indeed, far richer than anything the sad, dusty-looking television images of famine or Bob Geldof's Band Aid concert had prepared me for. My goal was to explore the country's historical heart: the source of the Blue Nile, which once challenged many early European explorers, Bahar Dar on Lake Tana, the castle city of Gondar, Lalibela with its rock-hewn churches and the mysterious town of Axum. This would take me on a clockwise route through the Eastern Highlands, starting at Lake Tana and ending at Axum. It is an area with the longest documented history in sub-Saharan Africa and, I was to discover, a history which made no distinction between politics, religion and the telling of a good, romantic tale. Indeed, for thousands of years, both church and state based their authority on a single story.

Some 3000 years ago, so the story goes, the powerful and beautiful Queen of Saba (Sheba) decided to visit King Solomon the Wise in Jerusalem. After a long journey from Axum she arrived (with a retinue of several thousand) and when Solomon saw her he was smitten. The noble queen wasn't prepared to jump into bed with him, but she was partial to an interesting challenge and Solomon the Wily set her one. She could sleep, unmolested, under his roof, he said, but if she took anything from the house he would have his way with her.

Perhaps stung by the insinuation that she might want his possessions, she agreed. That evening he held a banquet and offered her highly salted foods, then placed a bowl of water by her bedside and lay hidden, watching. Deep in the night she awoke, parched from the salt, and drank from the bowl, whereupon Solomon demanded his rights. Later that night, however, he dreamt that a great light, the divine presence, had left Israel and moved to Ethiopia.

The outcome of the adventure was the birth of Menelek I. He grew up with his mother at Axum but, on maturity, he insisted on meeting his father and travelled to Jerusalem. There he met Solomon and studied under him, becoming a star pupil and converting to Judaism. Some years later, however, he wished to return to his mother and Solomon was distraught, wanting him to remain, but eventually accepting his wishes.

At this point there is some dispute in the history. In Solomon's possession was the fabled Ark of the Covenant, the mysterious cask containing the Ten Commandments written on stone tablets by God and given to Moses. Some histories say Solomon gave it to Menelek, others that he and a group of young men filched it. According to the second version Solomon was enraged, but later realised that this had been implied in his dream and he forgave Menelek.

Since then, Ethiopians insist, the Ark has been housed in Axum, and it remains there to this day in an unobtrusive, grey-granite chapel guarded by a single, venerable priest and a

steel-spiked fence. But Menelek did more than bring home the Ark, copies of which form the holy of holies in each of Ethiopia's 22,000 or so churches. He also laid the foundations of a great dynasty which was to rule the country for the next 3000 years. Indeed, history records 97 rulers before Sheba and 237 after her, ending with Haile Selassie I, who was deposed in the communist takeover in 1974.

His removal from power by junior army officers and his ignoble death thus marked the end of an era stretching back nearly 4000 years.

While flying from Addis Ababa to Bahar Dar on Lake Tana, however, it was not history which preoccupied me but colour and form. As the patchwork quilt of tef, wheat and barley fields unfolded beneath the aircraft's wings I couldn't initially figure out what was missing. Then I realised what it was: there were no visible roads, not even jeep tracks. With 80 per cent of its people being rural peasants this was largely a nation which walked. Watching the rich green fields drifting slowly below me, though, I wondered how people in Ethiopia could possibly starve.

In Bahar Dar the next morning I met them in all their diversity. Stepping away from the minibus in this mêlée was like leaving a time capsule – I kept glancing back to make sure the vehicle didn't disappear. The market was a huge crush of people, most desperately poor, buying and selling the daily necessities of a life with few material comforts. Women sat along the lanes between stalls hawking spices, beans, nuts, salt, wool, garlic, spoons....

There was a whole spread of what looked like crude door locks, another of ladles, still another of highly-coloured skeins of wool. One man, sitting in a black puddle which spread around him, was decanting used engine oil into smaller containers for sale.

Skeletal men in white, hooded robes stood silently offering long, green gum poles; another repaired ancient umbrellas. Women offered balls of brightly coloured, hand-dyed wool or beautiful lengths of woven cloth which shimmered in the sun. A corner stall fixed bicycles, all of which looked beyond repair. Drifters from another planet, our little party of travellers attracted the curious, open stares of countless children. Women, unused to cameras, disappeared behind umbrellas or turned aside as I raised my lens. Some actually ran away, shouting in fright.

An old man in immaculate white sat on his haunches, haggling with a hawker over the price of a ladle. I dropped to one knee near them and looked through the camera's view-finder. They stopped and glared in my direction for a moment, then went on haggling. The shutter clicked and both scowled at me again, then continued. Twenty minutes later they were still at it: setting the right price for a ladle, it seemed, could become an honest morning's work.

This is how it must have been along the Nile for countless centuries – now there are bright plastic buckets and bicycles, but there's little other evidence of the 21st century.

Next day papyrus boats called *tankwas* plying Lake Tana – looking little different from those depicted on the tombs of the pharaohs – enhanced the feeling of timelessness. Our destination was the densely wooded Zege Peninsula and the monastery of Kidane Mihiret (there are also 37 islands on the lake, 20 of them sheltering monasteries). On the peninsula is a 700-year-old church, which turned out to be an emporium of surprises. Its huge, conical roof was covered with bright-blue plastic sheeting and at its centre was the Great Mystery, accessible only to the priests. I stepped onto an enclosed veranda encircling the building, its inner wall covered by long velvet curtains.

As I entered from the bright sunlight, the place gave me a feeling of brooding gloom, then the priest threw open the outer doors and rolled back the curtains. I was almost blinded by an explosion of colour: every surface from the floor to the ceiling six metres above and encircling the building, including doors and window frames, was covered in ancient, glowing icons, each one on a shimmering yellow background.

The tableau was so unexpected I staggered back against the outer wall, startled by the unexpected energy of the place.

Mary, baby Jesus, saints, demons, huge-eyed women, priests, dragons, headless creatures, bodiless birds and countless angels clamoured for attention: two thousand years of religious history in brilliant, Byzantine, technicolour graphics.

Outside, a crowd which had assembled for a funeral chanted and the principal mourners wailed to the thrum of a barrel-sized drum and tinkling cymbals. I was, quite literally, entranced; the ordinary dissolved into the images and rhythms of a world beyond time.

The following day, a stiff walk to the Blue Nile Falls from the village of Tissisat, just south of Bahar Dar, brought me back to earth. Here the great river, brown after the summer rains, plunged into a gorge along about a kilometre of cliff edge. The great volume of falling water and the spray make these falls remarkably similar to Victoria Falls, if not quite as impressive.

The Scottish explorer James Bruce, who came upon the falls in 1770, wrote that the river 'fell in one sheet of water with a force and a noise that was truly terrible and which stunned me and made me, for a time, perfectly dizzy'.

In the nearby village we met the true face of Ethiopian poverty: its children. As we walked their soft voices followed us everywhere: 'Hello. What's your name? I'm a student. Give me your address. Do you have a birr [money] for me? A pen?' They shadowed us, half a pace away, speaking incessantly. In the beginning they were sweet, but they were soon dubbed 'Velcro Kids' and finally, unkindly, simply 'Velcro'. In more remote areas their condition was often pitiable, their clothing mere rags and their eyes rimmed with feeding flies. But their patter never varied: 'A birr? A pen? Your address?' At the airport, as we headed north, the porters took up their refrain.

In the late afternoon sun the rolling green hills surrounding Gondar, north of Lake Tana in the foothills of the Simien Mountains, shone like emeralds. Looking down from the high road which connects the town to the lake, it occurred to me that if I had been a hunter-gatherer who chose to be rid of the old ways, it is here that I would have dropped my spears and picked up a hoe to begin village life. Streams flowed gently among the protective hills; valleys invited cultivation and hilltops offered protection from invaders.

Above the town the hillsides were a watercolourist's delight; a patchwork of barley, wheat and bean fields in complementary shades of green which, on their own, were a delight to the eye. But after the summer rains almost every space which was not field, forest or hamlet shimmered with bright yellow *adey abeba* (*Bidens macroptera* – called the mother of flowers). The effect was one of almost impossible beauty: if you painted it, few would believe you had actually seen it that way.

The town did not let me down either. At its edges temporary shelters of grass and sticks hovered beside more solid mud dwellings. Further towards the town centre more formal, but still ancient, buildings peered gently over streets filled with the hubbub of bartering and bickering merchants while sheep, cows and goats, seemingly ownerless, wandered round or leaned up against walls, seeking shade.

On the hillsides all about, dark castles glowered over massive stone perimeter walls and in the town centre a bright, plastic Mobil sign hovered over a crazy assortment of trucks, buses and taxis, many looking as though they'd just been exhumed from the depths of a scrap heap.

This was a town with its head (judging from the vehicles) in the 1960s, and its roots in the early 17th century. Gondar's rise to prominence under Emperor Fasilidas occurred about a century after Ethiopian Christendom had come close to total destruction at the hand of the Islamic warlord Ahmed Gragn, whose forces swept in from the east in 1528. Its establishment by Fasilidas in 1636 marked an important turning point in Ethiopian history and it soon emerged as the country's political, religious, commercial and cultural centre. When James Bruce came across Gondar in the 18th century it contained, he estimated, about 10,000 families.

Gondar has been called the Camelot of Africa, and for good reason. Stepping into the Royal Enclosure with its five castles, raised walkways and connecting tunnels, you'd be excused for thinking you were somewhere in medieval Europe. I could almost hear the roar of the crowd urging on jousting knights thundering across the generous green lawns. The effect was disorienting.

The first Gondarian castles were said to have been designed by master craftsmen from India, Greece, Portugal and Axum for the emperors Fasil, Yohannes I and his son, Iyasu. In the palace of Iyasu II, Bruce found mirrors from Venice set in gilt frames, a ceiling covered with gold leaf and precious stones, pictures and wooden boxes inset with ivory. The enclosure also contained the royal archives and a sauna, but a number of buildings were badly damaged in 1941 when Britain bombed the Italian headquarters which had been set up within the compound.

On the outskirts of the town is Faisal's Pool, a large, sunken bathing pool which surrounds a two-storey building thought to have been Fasil's second residence, and northwest of the town is the extraordinary Church of Debre Birhan Selassie. Built during the reign of Yohannes I, it is among the most beautiful churches in Ethiopia.

Many of Gondar's churches were destroyed in the 19th century Mahdist War by the Dervish of Sudan, but Debre Birhan Selassie, so the story goes, was saved by a swarm of bees. Its roof is decorated with the faces of 80 angels on the customary yellow background and the walls are covered by startling frescoes, the work of 17th-century artist Haile Meskel. Gondar is a good starting point for two adventures: climbing the Simien Mountains and visiting the rock-hewn churches of Lalibela. For us, Lalibela beckoned.

After seemingly endless baggage checks and body searches (batteries and pocket knives were temporarily confiscated and camera tripods regarded with suspicion) we sat on the grubby veranda of Gondar Airport, swatting flies as the Ethiopian Airlines Twin Otter was fitted with a new fuel pump. Finally the 18-seater lifted off the dusty runway and headed east, flying low over the patchwork fields and rugged mountains of the highlands.

There's a delightful informality about these internal flights: 'There's a hilltop monastery,' called the pilot. 'We're going in.'

The aircraft dived down between two mountains and snaked up a valley. The monastery appeared at wing-tip height as cameras clicked. Minutes later Lalibela came into sight, a dusty-looking village crowning a flat-topped mountain.

The plane banked steeply, circling our destination, and the first of the rock-hewn churches appeared: the roof was in the shape of a Greek cross capping a tall, symmetrical building in a large, square pit.

In Lalibela there are 13 churches, all carved into the larval rock and connected by tunnels. At ground level these structures are astounding. Many of the surrounding walls have 'priest holes' from which venerable men, magnificently attired in purple and yellow, appeared as we passed. One niche still contained the mummified bodies, bones and skulls of pilgrims who, we were told, 'drank the water of the Jordan and then died there'.

The sheer audacity of these huge buildings is head-spinning. They were constructed early in the 12th century under the direction of King Lalibela who, as a young man, so the story goes, had been transported to three different heavens. There God reputedly told him to build churches, the like of which the world had never before seen, and gave him the plans. What was required was no less than the creation of a 'new Jerusalem' in Africa. The

churches he built, after being crowned king, cluster round a deep gash called River Jordan, which serves as a drain for the structures when it rains.

The engineering of the complex – at a time when building technology was but hammers, chisels and wheelbarrows – is as confounding as the pyramids of Egypt. Unlike a conventional building constructed from the ground up, these had to be conceived in their entirety from the top down. Roofs were carved into the rock, then water channels and parapets, followed by the walls complete with windows and doors, as tons of rock were hauled out of the pits to make way for the work. Having hacked to the base of the structures, builders then had to carve into them, creating column supports as they progressed, then proceed upwards, hollowing out the structures to exactly replicate the walls and barrel vaults of more conventional churches.

Only at floor level were the connecting tunnels carved, so all the rubble had to be hauled up and out of the pits for removal. When you consider that some of these pits are 12 metres deep, the scale of this undertaking becomes apparent. Local legend has it that King Lalibela's team worked on the structures by day and angels continued their work by night. Given that all 13 churches were said to have been built within 26 years, that's a compelling explanation. The entire complex is, in fact, a single sculpture, a prayer in stone carved into the mountain.

The churches contain ancient and priceless paintings, crosses, crowns and other relics – many dating back 900 years. Much was evidently stolen during the rule of Mengistu (1974–1991) and in 1997 the most sacred object, a seven-kilogram gold cross said to have magical healing powers, disappeared from Beta Ghiorgis, the most famous of the rock-hewn churches.

These structures are not empty tourist attractions, but are living churches. We had to wait for services to end and, sometimes, sidled in to listen to sonorous chanting and smell the heady incense. Often we made way for priests scurrying through the tunnels on their daily business. For a small donation to church funds, priests in gloriously coloured robes would pose patiently with some or other sacred golden object as we photographed them.

In one church, Golgota, is Lalibela's tomb; in Beta Ghiorgis is a large wooden box with secret wooden screws, which is reputed to have contained the king's sacred books, crosses and other treasures. The latter church is dedicated to St George and has many paintings of the stern knight, helpless maidens and nasty-looking dragons.

Further north, not far from Eritrea and in the province of Tigre, lies Axum. Even in a country of ever-present antiquity there was something strange about the place: eerie, ancient. Camels, buses, 4x4s, cattle, people and donkeys mingled comfortably in wide streets lined with an assortment of general dealers, drug shops, ethnic clothing makers, silversmiths, bicycle-repair shops and houses.

It initially seemed to be a normal Ethiopian town until I glanced up Obelisk Road. Leaning gently to one side was a 23-metre-high stele of intricately carved rock, glinting in the hot midday sun. It's a single block of hewn granite thought to have been erected about 2000 years ago by King Ezana. Weighing around 400 tons, it was transported from a quarry many kilometres distant, possibly by using elephants and rollers. It's not known how the stele was erected, particularly as it is embedded in a base stone which may have required the giant carving to be lifted clear of the ground and dropped into place. Alternatively, the stele could have been tipped into place and the base slipped over it like a collar, but the size of the base makes this technique equally amazing.

There are many other smaller stelae around, all aligned towards the rising sun. But the largest stele, credited to the third-century King Ramhai, now lies shattered on the ground. The pieces weigh 500 tons, are decorated with a door and 12 windows and would have stood 33 metres high – it must have come down with a terrific thump. A 26-metre stele was looted by Mussolini in 1937 and now stands on a piazza in Rome – a bone of much contention in Axum.

Nearby the fallen obelisk is Ramhai's tomb, consisting of 12 underground vaults. It's constructed of large blocks of granite held together by metal pins and the precision of the masonry demands new respect for its long-dead stone masons.

Just across the road is a huge, unattractive, modern church which overshadows a compound enclosing a castle-like building and the ruins of several other churches, all called St Mary Zion Church, and the rather unattractive little chapel said to contain the Ark of the Covenant.

The ancient Ethiopians were followers of Judaism and there is speculation that they are the so-called 'lost tribe' of Israel. Christianity is thought to have arrived as early as the first century, during the reign of Queen Candace, after her treasurer was baptised at Gaza by the apostle Philip. The moment is recorded in Acts 8:26: 'An angel of the Lord spake to Philip saying: "Arise and go south to the road that descends from Jerusalem to Gaza." And he arose and went; and behold, there was an Ethiopian eunuch, a court official of Candace, Queen of the Ethiopians, who was in charge of her treasure, and had come to Jerusalem to worship … they both went down into the water, Philip as well as the eunuch, and he baptised him.'

It was only four centuries later, under Emperor Ezana, that Christianity was made the official religion of Ethiopia. But the early conversions of Menelek to Judaism, and Candace and Ezana to Christianity – and the profound effect this had on their respective cultures – suggest that Ethiopia has one of the longest unbroken histories of Judaeo-Christianity in the world.

Near the stele field is Queen Sheba's bathing pool (which now seems to serve as the local laundry), and the ruins of her palace – with evidence of 50 rooms, an elaborate drainage system and a fine kitchen – are three kilometres out of town. An enthusiastic guide from the National Travel Organisation insisted we see the museum and King Kaleb's Palace; and he was right. The former contains remarkable artefacts which speak of a gracious civilisation with highly skilled craftsmen, and the latter is said to be connected to the Red Sea port of Adulus – 130 kilometres away – by a tunnel built by the king to move his troops. Local legend has it that two priests once tried to make the underground journey and never returned. Nobody has tried it since.

Sitting on the base of a stele in the cool, clear pre-dawn of my last day in Axum, I looked down at my amulet and recalled my discussion with Marishet Dires – and remembered he'd left me the task of finding the symbolic meaning of red.

As the little shops began to open their doors I wandered along Obelisk Road and was greeted warmly by Alganesh Asgedom, whom I'd met the day before.

'You look thoughtful. What's the matter?' she asked.

Alganesh wasn't the sort of person to be evasive with, so I told her the puzzle I had about the colour red.

'It's the people!' she replied.

I glanced at her honey-brown complexion and must have looked rather doubtful.

'Have you been to a coffee ceremony?' she asked, seeming to re-track the conversation. When I shook my head she said: 'That may solve your problem. I'll ask Alem....'

'Please sit down,' said Alem Tsehay, indicating a stool opposite her. She was a hairdresser and, as are many Ethiopians, extremely beautiful. Her hair was tightly braided across her head and spread out across her shoulders in a thick mane of tight black curls. Between us was a small brazier containing hot coals, a tiny paraffin stove, a mortar and pestle, a bulbous pot and a silver tray on which were two cups, a bag of roasted coffee beans and a small mound of rock incense. Beneath all this was a mat of fresh eucalyptus leaves.

Alem ground the beans, humming softly, then poured them down the pot spout. The aroma of fresh coffee filled the room, but before my nose could grow accustomed to it she placed a coal in a small container and dribbled some incense over it. Smoke rose and its delicious scent, mixed with the aroma of coffee and eucalyptus, made my head swim.

A few minutes later rich black coffee was poured over sugar lumps in the cups. Alem handed me a cup and lifted the other in a shy toast. The taste was rich and sweet, and I succumbed to a feeling of contentment.

I sighed and Alem smiled, her large eyes twinkling, but neither of us spoke. With the cups drained, the ceremony was over. As I stood up to leave I handed her ten birr but she pushed my hand away: this was simple friendship, money had no place here.

As the aroma of coffee and incense trailed me out the door I realised that my search for the final colour was indeed over. Alganesh had been right: red represented the warm, friendly heart of the Ethiopian people.

Into the sands of silence

No bird greeted the dawn. There was not a leaf to shimmer in the slanting rays, no breeze to blow it, no insect to chirr, no sound at all.

As the yellow light probed between sun-blackened, time-sculpted rocks of the Akakus Mountains it set the peach-pink sand aglow. When I adjusted my position, a small rivulet of sand skidded down the dune face, hissing loudly in my silence-shocked ears.

If you placed your finger on a map of Africa a bit north of the midpoint between the coasts of Libya and Nigeria, Mauritania and Eritrea, you'd be pointing to the spot where I awaited the sun: right in the middle of the Sahara. It was a very strange place to be. It was an even stranger place to begin a hunt for savanna giraffe, ibex and elephant. And Bushmen.

When I returned to camp after listening to the desert's unnerving stillness, the camels were well rested and the Tuareg guides had breakfast simmering. It would soon be time to travel and, hopefully, begin to unravel a thread in the history of Africa's most mysterious people.

The Sahara had not always been this empty. A growing body of research suggests that some 6000 years ago – a mere yesterday in geological time – it was savanna fed by long, meandering rivers. Petrified forest vegetation has been unearthed. In the Murzuq Sand Sea of south-western Libya the bones of crocodiles, hippos, elephants and antelope have been found.

Until the great desiccation of North Africa, caused by seasonal shifts which are still only partly understood, giraffes munched on acacia trees along now-long-dead rivers. And in rock overhangs Neolithic artists ground pigments and painted the animals they hunted and the strange, other-worldly visions induced by trance dances. The oldest bones yet discovered in the Sahara belonged not to Negroid or Arab people but, astoundingly, to the oldest of all African inhabitants – Bushmen.

You don't have to have a reason to travel to Central Sahara, just a touch of madness. Simply to be there is reason enough. But the possibility that the art was of Neolithic San origin was irresistibly intriguing.

Three months earlier, being in the Sahara had seemed impossible. The United Nations embargo on flights to Libya had only recently been lifted and tourism in that country was embryonic. Visas weren't exactly a problem, they simply took time and had to be okayed by officials in Tripoli.

The first plane booking had to be cancelled because the visas hadn't arrived. Finally we touched down in Libya but, as it was Ramadan, all flights out were booked up for a month. To get out we'd have to trek to Tunisia and fly from Tunis. My colleague Robyn Daly and I had flown up the Nile, and on to Istanbul, then over a snow-cloaked Mount Olympus to Tripoli. The omens appeared auspicious.

Tripoli, Libya's capital, was founded by the Phoenicians, fell to the Nubians, was built to magnificence by the Romans (who named it Oea), sacked by the Vandals, and invaded by Arabs; then it fell to the Turks, and then the Italians – well, you get the picture.

Leaving it was a relief. It has an atmospheric Old Quarter, some really tasteless newer edifices and insane traffic. It's hectically urban. Less than 100 kilometres south, though, was the unsettling but exciting presence of the brooding Sahara.

We set the odometer of the Kia minibus to zero and headed for Ghadamis. The air was sharp and the shimmering dome of the sky matched the blue of my backpack. Some 70 kilometres south of the coast the terrain changed to flat scrub desert, relieved occasionally by hardy fig and, oddly, Australian gum trees.

'Camel grazing,' commented our guide, Sherif Shebani of Coast and Desert Tours. 'Nothing much else out here.'

At first the mountains seemed unreal, a mirage balancing on the arrow point of the road ahead. But they gradually resolved into the Western Mountains, Jabal Nafusah, a chain which begins as the Atlas Mountains in Morocco and stretches clear across Algeria, ending in the sea at the ancient Roman city of Leptis Magna, east of Tripoli.

These craggy peaks, rising nearly a kilometre into the sky, are an escarpment which seems to dam the great sand sea. Along this range live the Berber people – forced there by Arab invasions which spread westwards from Egypt some 1300 years ago, and hedged in by the southern desert.

We hairpinned up Jabal Nafusah below the town of Nalut and under the glowering stare of what seemed to be a castle. It turned out to be a *ksar* – a 14th-century grain warehouse and olive press. Looking like the life works of a giant mud wasp, the place was a bewildering warren of grain 'cells' stacked all atop each other and accessed by now-crumbling stairs and ledges. Holes and ducts kept the bins cool.

Nalut is a Berber town, perched on the lip of the crumbling escarpment like Cubist flotsam on the shore of a gravel ocean. Some 30 kilometres south of the town the first dunes appeared – mounds of rilled orange sand. As we rolled ever southwards, wraiths of sand began to drift across the road, like fingers testing the hot tarmac surface. They were fed by peach-coloured dunes which had munched up the last of the scrub.

The camels, when they appeared, seemed entirely appropriate. We stopped, spellbound, as about 150 of the strange, complaining creatures streamed past, the slanting sun flaring silvery auras off their shaggy coats.

Their Tuareg herdsman shook my hand, then touched his chest.

'Salaam alaikum.'

'Wa-alaikum salaam,' I replied.

His face was the colour of the dunes and his eyes seemed to bore through mine to some ancient part of my brain. I sat, watching his departing back, not a little shaken by the contact.

Instead of the anticipated dunes, though, we rolled out onto a great gravel desert, varnished to an eerie sheen by wind-blown sand and stretching as far as the eye could see. To the west lay Tunisia and Algeria, to the east the trackless nothing of the Tarabulus region. We are so accustomed to human ownership and use of the planet's surface that hundreds upon hundreds of kilometres of virtually untouched emptiness evokes a strange lightness of heart. Like the Antarctic, the Sahara is one of the greatest wilderness areas on earth. Its sheer hostility has preserved it for the very few who know and respect its ways.

Beyond a tatty little oasis named Darj, darkness wrapped us in introspection. We'd been travelling almost dead straight for hundreds of kilometres.

'There are huge dunes here,' Sherif commented. But all we saw along the tunnel of headlights was the occasional moth and a fleet-footed white jerboa, reminding us that even out here life still maintained a tenuous hold.

After the desolation of the desert the guesthouse in Ghadamis, Villa Otman Hashaishe, was a delight. A small restaurant nearby provided a fine meal, the shower was hot and the beds comfortable. I got a sense of what an oasis must feel like to a traveller after weeks on a caravan trek.

Ghadamis is described as the Jewel of the Desert and its heart is an artesian well which has provided water for thousands of years. The old part of the town – being restored by Unesco – is an ingenious system of cool tunnels through a warren of multiple-storeyed houses and mosques. Our Ghadamis guide, Mohamed Ali Kredn, was born in the old quarter and led us round unerringly. Without him we'd have been hopelessly lost inside a minute.

We left Ghadamis before sunrise under a full orange moon. The lights of the town soon disappeared and the dunes, rising and falling in the moonlight, looked like mid-ocean rollers. Dawn arrived quite suddenly in the moisture-leeched air. A glow on the horizon, then a ripple of bright gold which jiggled and formed into an enormous ball of fire dead ahead. The moon, like a pale lady afraid of the heat, slipped below the opposite horizon and was gone.

The day offered a sight both bleak and thrilling. The dunes had receded and we were crossing the Al Hammadah, a gravel desert so featureless that a molehill would have been an object worth studying. In every direction was a sort of biological and zoological nihilism, with the horizon as a near-straight line marked only by a colour change between earth and sky. The arrow-straight road, silvered by the rising sun, seemed to leak sky into a widening flow around us and swallowed it back up behind our humming vehicle. The day's goal: 1100 kilometres of absolute nothing. The boredom which this kind of road induces is an almost tangible thing. Your mind goes numb before the great emptiness, recoils upon itself and very soon begins to work in dream mode.

At an oasis named Ash Shwayrif the road veered south towards Sabha, the largest town in southern Libya. Brave bushes, strung like green pearls along dry wadis, were a welcome relief from the smashed-rock landscape. Future colonists destined for Mars could spend time in these wastelands getting themselves acclimatised.

I was so numbed I only focused on the trucks when one sped past us loaded with onions and smelling delicious. Others followed, carrying wheat, maize and watermelons, all heading out of the wasteland towards the coast. Then came the fields of Sabha and the out-of-place zik-zik of water sprinklers. The town wasn't the dusty desert place I'd expected: the streets were lined with trees and hedges and prosperity was obvious. The key to this mystery is artesian wells, dug thousands of years ago, and still producing the liquid of life in abundance. We pulled in to a smart restaurant for hamburgers, kebabs and fruit nectar. I hoped we weren't eating camel.

From Sabha the road snaked along a wide valley with a harsh, high escarpment to the south and the edge of the massive Azzallaf Erg (sand sea) to the north. But, for more than 200 kilometres, the valley floor was covered with gardens and dotted with water towers, pines, palm and casuarinas. It didn't fit my Sahara stereotype.

We turned into Africa Camp at Ubari some 13 hours after leaving Ghadamis. It was an attractive little tented camp with a restaurant at the foot of pink dunes which stretched from east to west as far as we could see. As night fell I trekked over a dune at least 100 metres high and settled on the powder-soft sand to await the moon. A large owl glided past. The silence was profound, and if I had any travel tension it soon leaked away into the sand. Perhaps I sat there an hour, maybe two. Forty days and forty nights would have been just fine.

From Ubari we headed west along the foot of *mesak* (mesa) mountains. The dunes receded and we were once again on a sand sea. As we neared Al Awaynat, the desert turned from lemon to slate. Dunes occasionally appeared on the horizon, then drifted out of sight. In all that expanse there was nothing but pebbles, gravel and sand. When your eyes beg for variation, it's surprising how many colours you can pick out of this stark geography.

We swapped the Kia for a Toyota Land Cruiser in Al Awaynat and headed dead south, following tracks towards the Akakus Mountains. The sun was low and when the foothills appeared they seemed to be covered in forest. But it was an illusion – out there was nothing but black rock and yellow sand.

Without road signs, obvious features or even tracks, the only way I can explain how we found the Tuareg camel men is to say that our Toyota driver was also Targui. The desert men were camped in a sandy depression among crazy-shaped boulders. Their camels were hob-tied but looked placid and – if a camel has the capacity – happy.

Raia Abdul Alrhman Embarak greeted us courteously, shaking hands and touching his breast with the proffered hand. He was a desert-wizened man with clear, smiling eyes above his ever-present nose veil, known thereabouts as a litham. But under his cloak you sensed steel. A fire was going and we were soon eating sand-baked bread and delicious Tuareg soup.

'Camels', said Raia between mouthfuls, 'are my life.' His people have dominated Central Sahara for centuries as raiders and caravan riders and they are still the desert's greatest fighters – true knights of the great sand ergs. As a youngster, Raia had crossed from Ghat in Libya to Niger with a caravan of dates. These days he does camel business in the Akakus, carrying archaeologists and occasional tourists.

Next morning he brought the camels down on their bellies ready to be ridden. I swung my leg over the camel's back, nearly impaling my calf on the spiked saddle. Raia yelled something at me and Sherif translated: 'He says, grab the hair on the camel's hump behind you or you'll break your teeth on the pommel when it gets up.'

I made a grab as the beast came up, backside first, then gave a mighty shove with its front knees. This threw me backwards as the camel came aloft. The saddle spikes, I figured, must be a way of separating the Targui from the tourists.

We set off for the deep crags and valleys of Akakus. After several hours of travelling we turned up a wide wadi which led directly into the mountains. High walls of sandstone closed in as we lumbered up a virtual sand highway. The surrounding crags had the appearance of hammered sea cliffs. Wind-driven sand and time had transformed cracks and fissures into yawning caves, arches and canyons.

We finally dismounted near an overhang and gaped in wonder. The wall was covered in rock art. Here were gangly giraffes, elephants, antelopes and stretched, skinny people. In some scenes men with bows and arrows with hunting dogs pursued walia ibex, in others women braided hair or clapped their hands. Further up the valley was a trance dance conducted by foot-stamping and Bushman-like half-human half-animal therianthropes. On the floor were tiny arrow heads. Had they once carried poison? At another site was a huge, perfectly proportioned elephant, and at still another were more recent paintings of camels and even the chariots of the ancient desert people known as Garamantes.

Who had painted these pictures? And when? The questions hung in the silence of the desert, unanswered. We do not yet know for sure. Their style, though, was recognisable. I'd seen it in many caves and overhangs at the southern end of the continent.

It would be incorrect to say that the trip back to the coast was an anticlimax. We went by a different route and saw other places: the desolate oasis of Brak, the flower-filled Berber town of Ghariyan, the ancient Roman city of Sabratah....

By degrees the healing silences of the sand ergs were replaced by the bump and chatter of urban life. But back in the silent valleys of Akakus questions remained. Had the Bushmen once been masters of all Africa? Was it they who had crossed the land bridge into Europe? Are we all their descendants? The evidence would need more work to be conclusive. But it was compelling.

One thing is for sure, if some of the extraordinary rock art in those mountain galleries was created by the San, they were certainly great travellers.

The homeliest homes in the loneliest sea

At five o'clock each morning Vanessa Lavarello tramps down the bumpy road to milk her cows. At the edge of the field she meets her mum, Judy, and her dad, Ken, who has some buckets of old potatoes to keep the cows occupied while the two women milk.

At the gate Vanessa calls: 'Here, Blackie. Come on, Blackie.' A cow obediently breaks from the herd and trots up to provide the day's supply. The women are dexterous, using one hand to squeeze the fresh milk into a jug held in the other. Some sheep wander over, looking a bit sleepy at the early intrusion, and a fuss of ducks set up a cluck in the brook below the gate.

Given the deep green fields and the people's rich accents, this could be taking place in some forgotten field that is forever England, except that at the edge of the field rises the smashed savagery of a volcano and behind the milkmaids is a village sheltering the remotest permanent human community on earth.

Tristan da Cunha, a dot on the map between South Africa and Uruguay, is the exposed top of an active volcano situated on the deep Mid-Atlantic Ridge. From base to crater it's 5500 metres – nearly as high as Mount Kilimanjaro.

With a hope and a prayer, the little village of Edinburgh – housing about 280 people plus their cattle, sheep, pigs, ducks, chickens, collie dogs and 'tater patches – clings to its northern skirts. All the houses face resolutely towards the wide, empty sea. The volcano, behind them, is another matter.

In August 1961 a series of tremors began shaking the settlement. When the administrator radioed this news to vulcanologists in England, they assured him it was a 'minor settling' along a possible fault line. Tristanians, with traditional stoicism about what nature could dish up, simply accepted the incessant shocks which followed for another two months.

Then, one Sunday, a really big thump nearly destroyed the church during evensong. According to the island administrator, Peter Wheeler, 'The walls heaved, the floor trembled and for a sickening second the roof threatened to cave in.'

Islanders dispatched to nearby Nightingale Island found no shocks occurring there and, more ominously, neither were they happening in other parts of Tristan. Edinburgh, it seemed, was the epicentre. Then the cliffs above the settlement began to give way, killing a cow and panicking sheep. A strange bubble of rock appeared in the pasture just east of the houses and swelled at the rate of about one-and-a-half metres an hour. The shocks became almost continuous and, according to resident Willie Repetto, stirred the earth 'like a plough moving the stones and rocks'.

Remembering Krakatoa, the East Indian island which exploded in 1883 killing 36,000 people, the islanders hastily packed what they could and trekked to the 'tater patches west of the settlement and thence, by canvas-covered longboats, to Nightingale Island. By good fortune they were plucked from this tiny refuge by a passing Dutch liner, *Tjisadane*, transported to Cape Town and then, by *Stirling Castle*, to England. By then the volcano was belching sulphur and spewing lava. A British frigate, HMS *Leopard*, arrived in time to fill some cartons with what possessions could be hastily packed and to shoot the dogs to prevent them from savaging sheep, and then it sped off to safety.

After about two years the islanders, having survived bitter English winters, voted to return home. When a reporter suggested they'd be returning to a hard life, old Martha Rogers replied, 'It is a hard life. But we-all doesn't mind. We doesn't get run over by no motorcars on Tristan. And nobody doesn't murder nobody.'

::

HMS *St Helena* arrived off Edinburgh village on a clear blue day in a flurry of swooping albatrosses and inquisitive shearwaters. The islanders – 40 years on and still vitally dependent on ships – were soon alongside in their tough little boats to ferry us ashore. The only sign of the eruption was a scar of black lava slicing across the eastern cow pasture and into the sea. Somewhere under it, swallowed whole, was the old crayfish factory.

The little harbour and the hill above it were crowded with onlookers – many of them shy women in bright print dresses, and their less restrained but still respectful children. There can be few places in the world where the arrival of a ship stops an entire town in its tracks.

Vanessa Lavarello, who, with husband John, was to be my host while on the island, was waiting under a 'Welcome to Tristan da Cunha' sign with a broad smile. Like most Tristanians she was warm but reticent, needing to be coaxed into conversation.

Vanessa's a direct descendant of the island's first permanent settler, Corporal William Glass from Scotland, who relocated his wife and children there in 1816. But with only seven family names on the island – all derived from 18th-century settlers or shipwrecked sailors – that's probably true of almost everybody on Tristan. The island's family tree, drawn up by writer Allan Crawford in the 1980s, looks more like a piece of delicately interwoven fabric than an ever-branching oak.

We strolled up through the pretty, rather haphazard village with its bumpy tracks, neat, picture-book buildings, black lava walls, spiky New Zealand flax hedges, bright clusters of hydrangeas and perky black-and-white collies defending their territories on the generous grass verges. Unlike the older houses, which had the appearance of being suspended between rough, stone bookend gables, Vanessa's was modern but with the same cottage feel. At the edge of the field behind it were sharply angled scree slopes scarred by black 'gulches'. Above them were almost vertical grey and black ramparts rising around 600 metres to the Base, a high plateau encircling the 2060-metre volcano. Along the skyline – looking more like swallows, given the vast scale of the cliffs – wheeled thousands of yellow-nosed and sooty albatrosses.

::

Tristan was discovered in 1506 by the Portuguese navigator Tristão da Cunha, who did not land, but named the island after himself. Then in 1811 Jonathan Lambert from the United States of America – probably a pirate – landed and declared himself emperor, but he disappeared under mysterious circumstances during a fishing expedition with his mates. Five years later Britain, fearing the French would use the island as a base from which to rescue Napoleon from exile on St Helena, established a garrison on Tristan. When this was withdrawn after a year, Corporal Glass, who'd brought his wife along, remained behind to found the civilian community.

In the days of sailing ships, the Atlantic's winds favoured the island with visitors and, quite often, wrecks, which provided useful wood for construction (and survivors to swell the gene pool). It is seldom appreciated that the best way to sail round the Cape – a route discovered by plucky Portuguese mariners – was to catch the north-easterlies towards

Brazil, then ride the south-westerlies back to Africa along the low latitudes around Tristan. When steam replaced sail, the island community was thrown into crisis, often with no ships calling for years.

Until the arrival of a naval signalling station during the Second World War, there was no money on the island. A person's wealth was measured by the number of potatoes they harvested. The first Tristanian postage stamp had printed on it: 'Local Value 4 Potatoes'.

As remote destinations go, few can equal this tiny circular island. The nearest mainland is the Western Cape, 1800 nautical miles away. It has no airstrip, is only a few degrees above the Roaring Forties and can be accessed only by ship. The passenger vessel RMS *St Helena* visits but once a year, and the island's only regular links with the outside world are a satellite phone and the coming and going of fishing boats belonging to the South African-based 'crawfish' factory. If the crayfish ever run out and if the island of St Helena builds an airstrip, making sea voyages by the RMS *St Helena* uneconomical, Tristanians may not only be the remotest, but also the most abandoned community on earth.

The volcano also remains an unknown quantity. The Tristan group of islands, together with St Helena, Ascension and the Azores, are all on the rim of the Mid-Atlantic Trench, an undersea gash – caused by continental drift – which stretches from Bouvetøya Island just off the Antarctic icepack through Iceland to the Greenland Sea.

When I asked Inspector Conrad Glass – the island's only policeman – whether all this concerned him, he gave me a practical Tristanian answer: 'Well, you can't go round all day worryin' about these things, you know.'

::

Day two dawned calm and blue – uncharacteristically so, many locals insisted. We took a ride out west to the potato patches – referred to simply as The Patches – and to The Bluff, crossing several gulches with names like Hottentot, Sandy and Molly. Here we stamped up to the rim of the plateau over tough grass, gritty black sand and, finally, clusters of tree ferns and *Philica arborea*, the island's only species of tree. Ropes attached to some of these were a great help up the steep parts.

The hike took several hours, but once over the rim it was worth it: the clouds had evaporated and the volcano loomed above us like a giant Basotho hat. In amongst the ferns, however, was the biggest attraction: albatross chicks. The one I approached sat bolt upright in a ground nest looking rather like a dog's water bowl and way too small for the metre-high mound of white fluff. The youngster had the fierce eyes of its species and a mean beak, which it snapped repeatedly in my direction.

The view from our perch was spectacular. Out to sea were Nightingale and Inaccessible islands, which, together with Gough Island further south, form the Greater Tristan Group. Far below were The Patches, neat black-walled gardens on an emerald green plain.

The walls of these individually owned plots are home to those great seafarers: rats. When they get out of hand, locals round up their collies and proclaim a Ratting Day. The latest *Tristan Times* reported prizes given for the team which caught the most rats (313) and the rat with the longest tail (28.4 centimetres).

On the way back to the village we passed several volcanic cones and a golf course which gave new meaning to the notion of 'rough'.

::

We travel, perhaps, to remind ourselves that we are, at heart, nomadic creatures, or maybe simply to peer into the lives of others the better to understand our own. Travelling to Tristan confounds both of these reasons.

Although few ships leave Cape Town heading west, and though the Southern Atlantic has a reputation for ripping sails or swallowing vessels whole, life aboard the RMS *St Helena* is rather like being in a country hotel on rockers. You're pampered and overfed for five days each way, and the spirit of nomadism is lulled to sleep by the long Atlantic rollers.

As for Tristanians, their lifestyle teaches only about a people's ability to lead normal lives in extraordinary circumstances. The island is no idyllic Arcadia. Educational opportunities are limited, youngsters hanker after experiences in the worlds across the sea and the choice of marriage partners is limited. A television dish, soon to be installed, may change aspirations and increase discontent; and Inspector Glass may one day find someone to overnight in his still-unused jail.

What Tristanians do show, however, is a simple, old-fashioned generosity of spirit – a rural sweetness almost untouched by the centuries.

As we loaded up and set sail for the green cliffs of Gough Island, the village lined up to watch us go. Before we reached their horizon, I imagined John Lavarello returning to his wall-building. Vanessa would stroll up to her warehouse job, then return home to clean her house after my departure, cook a bluefish pie and deep-fry some 'taters.

At five o'clock the next morning she'd be up to milk the cows, then return to her parents' house for a cup of tea and a chat about the coming and going of the ship. The volcano at their backs, an unpredictable black dragon, would continue to brew the way volcanoes do. Like the remote little community on its northern toe, it gives the impression of having time on its side.

Karoo dreaming

Long before dawn I would be coaxed out of bed and shepherded into the back seat of the car, still clutching my pillow. There I'd fall asleep again, with the tassels of the travelling blanket tickling my cheeks.

Hours later I would wake to the hum of the engine and the smell of egg-and-mayonnaise sandwiches. Up ahead the road would stretch out endlessly, while the side windows offered a featureless blur of brown veld and distant, flat-topped hills. We'd be going somewhere strange and exciting: Cradock, maybe, Graaff-Reinet, Molteno or some farm lost in the vastness of it all. But getting there seemed to stretch time like the rubber band trapping the grease-proof paper round my sandwich. I'd stare out the window at the cloud towers and vast blue sky, unsure whether I was awake or dreaming.

I once asked – I must have been about six – why the road went on for so long. I still remember my mother's reply: 'It's the Karoo, dear.' As far back as I can remember, the Karoo, that vast, flat tableland which comprises much of South Africa's interior, has reminded me of huge distances, slow-moving time and egg-and-mayonnaise sandwiches.

The sandwiches were absent, but all the other ingredients were in place as my son and I turned off the N1 at Matjiesfontein and headed for the distant Komsberge and the village of Sutherland. The road sped beneath our vehicle, but long before it reached the horizon all movement seemed to slow to zero. The speedometer told me we were moving, but we didn't seem to be going anywhere. It was an illusion, of course, because the village of Sutherland eventually hove into view. A couple of kilometres before reaching it, I turned off onto a secondary road and bumped along to Skurweberg Guest Farm.

'Hi, I'm Witjan,' said its owner, emerging from a shed, wiping his hands on a cloth and leaving me wondering if there had been a Jan of another colour in his early history. 'Let me show you the place.'

The guesthouse was a neat building fronted by a thick lawn looking incredibly green for the semi-desert surrounds. Witjan and Elsa van der Merwe whipped up beer and a braai. As bats hawked moths in the veranda light we talked about seeds, horse traps, Land-Rovers and the size of the Karoo. That night we tucked up to the sound of large, ripe peaches plopping onto the lawn outside the window.

Before dawn the next morning we were trussed up in Witjan's open Landy and heading for the Roggeveld Escarpment. One can coo over 4x4s, polish them, use them as status symbols or keep them in a garage until the family holiday. But there's nothing to beat hacking your way up a mountain in a tough workhorse you don't mind bashing. I can't imagine how we got there, but Witjan suddenly skidded to a halt a mere metre from the escarpment edge. The view was head-spinning.

To the south, at least 100 kilometres away, was the Witteberg range, the southernmost rim of the Karoo plateau. To the west – with the Teapot clearly visible – was the Cedarberg and east, perhaps 200 kilometres distant, were the Swartberge. Far below the valleys were still swathed in dawn shadow. Wisps of mist were beginning to rise from the stream beds. Somewhere, somehow, I'd seen this before. But the memory wouldn't surface.

That afternoon, with the silence of Skurweberg still ringing in my ears, we drove into Sutherland and found the silence unbroken. The place reminded me of a shootout scene from a John Wayne movie: two cowboys walking slowly towards each other, hands poised above their guns, as the rest of the townsfolk step behind walls and doorways, interested but silent. But in Sutherland the gunmen were absent.

We checked into The Cottage, run by Ridi Blom, who nudged my memory about the sort of guys I used to hang out with in the sixties. He showed me an Alpha Romeo he'd restored and a motorbike, on which he'd done every conversion imaginable. I guess, in the

Karoo, you need to be able to eat up kilometres. He runs a fine little guesthouse in a laid-back way. If you get him in the right mood he'll tell you the sort of filigree stories only a small town can generate.

Enquiring about places of interest round the village, we were directed – via the dominee who had the key – to the Van Wyk Louw Museum. This brilliant Afrikaans poet began life in Sutherland and his works now share the museum with the rather frugal pickings of former cabinet minister Adriaan Vlok and the more prolific paraphernalia of dam builder Sir Hendrik Olivier. But if you need something with more depth of field, Rudi can arrange a visit to the huge telescopes of the nearby astronomical observatory.

The temperature was starting to climb as we rolled out of town on the R356 and by 10h00 the horizon was jiggering with mirages.

'Would you like me to drive?' my son enquired.

'No, it's okay. I like driving these long stretches,' I countered.

'Well, would you mind if I slept in the back seat...?'

Fraserburg, when it finally appeared, turned out to be famous for its monsters. The story goes like this: some 250 million years ago, in the late Permian age, a huge river (which no longer exists) burst its banks and spilled muddy water onto a floodplain. When the water subsided large pools remained. Worms popped up, leaving squiggles in the sand, an aquatic arthropod wandered along, some fish left tail marks in the mud, then a few dinocephalians came stomping up to investigate. These duck-billed reptiles – up to three metres long – lumbered over the mud, followed by a heavily armoured bradysaurus.

The mud dried and the tracks would have eventually blown away. But a week or so later the river flooded again, covering them with a thin layer of what would later harden into sandstone. The trackway was eventually buried under maybe a few thousand metres of sediment; then, millions of years later it was exposed again along the spillway of a farmer's dam.

Today the Gansfontein Paleosurface is the village of Fraserburg's pride and joy, and in the village museum dinocephalians, diictodons and other creatures share space with, among other things, *boere* kitchenware, old village photographs and a Victorian pram.

Just outside is a curious old clocktower known as the Peperbus and a neat corbelled hut made entirely of stone. Some of these extraordinary round huts are national monuments, built by early settlers in the absence of wood. Why gravity doesn't claim their rock-lapped roofs is remarkable.

Later we dropped in to the local café for something to drink and a sandwich, but they didn't make sandwiches. When I asked the man at the till how things were these days, he said 90 per cent of the people in the village were over 70 and there were only three white kids in high school. We saw many happy school children and a good few adults under 70, but I guess when you're just passing through a village you can't expect a precise census. Fraserburg is the quintessential Karoo *dorpie* and we'd have liked to stay longer, but time and the road drew us onwards. Beyond the town my son switched on the radio and the tuner began to track for stations, the dial spinning uselessly through the FM bands. He had to switch it off to put it out of its hissing misery.

The Karoo system covers about three-quarters of South Africa and its early formation (the Dwyka Series) took shape as the silty bed of a huge inland lake. A glacial period lowered the basin floor by sheer weight, but when the ice melted, huge sand and mud masses filled the plains again, forming the coal-rich Ecca Series.

This was followed by a period of steady rain and a boom in animal and plant life. This period, captured in sedimentary rocks known as the Beaufort Series, has yielded the greatest number of fossils known to science. The present cycle is dry – the Karoo receives less that 250 millimetres of rain a year. Its name is derived from the San word *Kurú* which implies 'dry and harsh'. In 1812 the German explorer Lichtenstein (who later founded the Berlin Zoo) described its form rather well: 'There are large spaces which are perfect plains, but these are intermixed with eminences.'

Some fine eminences made their appearance along the R356 to Loxton. I stepped out of the car into the heat to photograph them and discovered the roof of the vehicle had been hiding the main performance: clouds. The flatter the land, of course, the bigger the sky. But blinding-white cumulo-nimbus towers in the Karoo-blue heavens suggested a canvas with its frame off somewhere in infinity.

Just when I had the feeling my real-life painting had no edge, the road took a sharp right turn and there was Loxton. If ever there's a village in South Africa which gives you the sense of being an oasis, this is it. Only the red-brick church spire peeps above the trees which clothe the area in a virtual woodland.

After the vast, dry plains, Loxton's lawns seem shockingly green. *Leiwater* flows along deep gutters beside the streets, to be sluiced into gardens according to a weekly roster. It would take no more than ten minutes to walk clear across the village. The houses are mainly old, well tended and unselfconsciously picturesque, the police station has no razor wire and the library is full of books. The only sound, mid-morning, was the chatter of fat sparrows.

Without romanticising the place, it is one of the most laid-back, pretty and desirable villages around in which to send down your rural roots. The same thought obviously crossed the minds of celebrated naturalist authors and researchers Chris and Tilde Stuart. They invited us in for some tea and chatted about their African–Arabian Wildlife Research Centre. As we left, a silver Rolls-Royce slid out of a garage down the road – someone off to fetch the morning paper. I suspect there's a lot more to Loxton than meets the eye.

We didn't overnight in the village but at Jakkalsdans, a 20,000-hectare farm and wildlife reserve nearby. It simply confirmed the unusualness of the area. Four generations of Van der Westhuizens have grown up there and each must have added something beautiful. Its gardens are park-like, the buildings should be in *Country Life* and the extensive guesthouse is packed with the sort of antiques it takes generations to acquire. Cala, of the fourth generation, was there to greet us.

Among his many stories over a fine evening meal was one about Danie van Graan of Loxton, who, in 1975, saw what he thought to be a caravan landing in his sheep camp. As he approached, three beings with high foreheads regarded him from the windows. Suddenly a beam hit him and his nose began to bleed so he backed off. Danie watched for a while, then his 'caravan' lifted off and disappeared in seconds.

As dawn touched the high pines we staggered away after a large farm breakfast and headed down the R381 towards Beaufort West. It's a beautiful road – or was I just relieved to see the endless plains broken by two mountain passes? The Molteno and Rosenberg passes ease you down from the Nuweveldberg Plateau through the Karoo National Park and into a town which seemed large after Loxton.

We pulled up at Beaufort West's elegant Clyde House and met its owner, Esther Smith. She's an art dealer, and was painting a large cloth, surrounded by pots of colour.

'I came here from the city to a teaching post,' she chuckled. 'I couldn't figure out this great nothing. Then one day I took a scrambler off to nowhere in particular. When I switched it off the silence wrapped round me. It was so alive. Then I understood.'

Beaufort West is an attractive little town with one abiding disadvantage – the main street is also the N1 highway between Cape Town and Johannesburg. This means that every day about 1500 articulated trucks and countless cars roar through.

After breakfast at Clyde House next morning we were sitting in the Getaway Bar of the Royal Hotel under the life-dealing air conditioner, listening to a bad remix of Bob Marley. We'd done the museum, full of Chris Barnard's awards and trinkets, checked out the surgeon's childhood home and explored the impressive Dutch Reformed Church. The heat was melting the tar outside. At that point Colin and Esther de Villiers came to our rescue.

'I'm in a Boerevereniging meeting right now,' said Colin when he rang. 'When I've finished we can go up to Badshoek.'

Their game farm, hunting lodge and guesthouse is nestled just below the Bain-built De Jager Pass. A friendly Labrador greeted us as we pulled up to what turned out to be another of those spectacular Karoo farmhouses. Colin built it onto an existing old stone prison, extending the walls upwards to create a mezzanine bedroom and deck section and outwards to form a large, friendly kitchen. The grand staircase is yellowwood, the ceilings are reed *brandsolder* and the roof is, extraordinarily, cool stone.

We jumped into Colin's Land-Rover and headed back up to the high country. The farm has an excellent 4x4 route up the skirts of the Nuweveld Mountains, offering spectacular views of the plains below.

Later, over drinks on the lawn, their daughter Ille introduced us to Roftie the tame crow. He's quite able to fly away, but chooses to stay, and entertained himself stealing ice out of Ille's glass of Coke. Dinner was *haute cuisine*, courtesy of Evelyn and her roaring coal stove.

That night we slept for the last time in the deep Karoo silence, waking to the thoughtful regard of a bat-eared fox.

On our way back through Beaufort West we finally found some egg-and-mayonnaise sandwiches, then set off down the long road to Cape Town. The smell of the sandwiches permeated the vehicle and we were unable to resist for long. We pulled over and scoffed the lot.

'Can I drive?' enquired my son as we prepared to hit the road again.

'Sure. Do you mind if I curl up in the back seat?'

'No problem.'

Contemplating yellowfish and shy elephants beneath the Tree of Idleness

The required weapons were a gold-ribbed hare's ear and a dark, bead-head nymph in tandem, linked by indeterminate lines to a four-piece, five-weight Dean Stream rod and Rim Fly reel. Mark Calverley is very precise about things like that. Our quarry was Natal yellowfish which, we hoped, were lurking in the Tugela just beyond the edge of the lawn.

I hadn't thrown a fly for more years than I was prepared to admit in that company, but we'd abseiled and hurtled down a foofee slide into the river, and the water was too low, just then, to shoot the rapids. So, as Mark put it, fishing was inevitable. We loaded rods, flies and people into his impossibly battered Suzuki jeep and bounded downstream to where the masters of caste deemed it correct and proper to fish.

In my book the KwaZulu-Natal Midlands should be green, rolling hills with pretty, self-satisfied towns, and atmospheric wraiths of mist. A sort of little England with the occasional cluster of Zulu huts. Down along the Tugela, however, we were in wild, dry valley bushveld where elephants browse, baboons scream at you and over-sized leopards rule the night.

We threaded our way among tambotie, red ivory, Transvaal lavender, white ironwood and marula trees to where the Suzuki could no longer get a tyre hold, and then hacked along the steep bank. On a large hot rock we assembled the rods, threaded the yellow line and tied on pretty flies. I was forced to admit that some advice was in order, so Roger Sheppard took me under his fin for a bit.

'It hurts when you hook your ear,' he offered, after showing me how to keep the line in the air until it needed to hit the water. Then he waded out into the swirling river.

In the soft, angled afternoon light he looked like the wish-you-were-there centrepiece of a whisky ad. His bright line curved across the background of a dark bank, water trailing from it like the glittering strings of a harp. If I was a yellowfish I'd have taken the fly for the sheer beauty of it.

My efforts were less inspiring. The fly flicked the water on both fore- and backstroke (how the devil do they keep it airborne?) and at one point it became acquainted with my hat, but fortunately not my ear. After about an hour of whipping the water we'd caught nothing, but that didn't seem to matter. The rods were simply a good excuse to be waist-deep in the swirling waters of one of South Africa's legendary rivers. When the sun hit the mountains we packed it in and bounded back happily to the warm embrace of Zingela Lodge.

Several decades ago, when Mark and his wife, Linda, were newly out of teachers' training college, they came to have a look at the defunct cattle farm that would one day become Zingela. The road was from hell, there were 22 gates and Linda was pregnant.

'If you want to live down there,' she told him, 'you do it by yourself!'

Mark loved the property, but they couldn't afford it. By 1983, when the place came on the market again, they could afford it and Mark promised to take down most of the gates, rip out the fences and turn it into a game conservancy. Linda assented and they put up a cooking tent to serve river rafters, who slept on the banks round the tent. Mark supported their dream hideaway through professional hunting, some of it on the farm.

Eventually, though, he got tired of running round Southern Africa with clients and guns. Several children and a desire to hunker down in paradise were a good argument for turning Zingela into something more than a riverside camp site.

Today habitation is still mostly under canvas, but there's more around than a cooking tent. Dining and lounging-around areas are under thatch, canvas and trees, there are rooms and

there are luxury lodges wrapped round granite boulders which stretch the concept of living under canvas to its limits. Zingela can accommodate up to 65 people.

Guests are met in Weenen, where their vehicles are left behind, and from there the adventure begins with a wild 4x4 ride to the river.

In summer Zingela is all about white-water rafting and rodeo kayaking. There's a 15-kilometre stretch of excellent rapids, including the Washing Machine, which, peaking at Grade 6, is the biggest commercially run rapid in South Africa. It has twice been host to the South African White-Water Championships.

As hot-doggers do their stuff in gurgling holes and grinding rapids, they're watched by nyala, bushbuck, kudu, blue wildebeest and the occasional leopard. The elephants, however, are far too shy to be spectators – they're probably the wildest herd in the country. In six months Mark has only spotted one of the possible 13 tuskers.

After breakfast the next morning Mark looked at the sky, sighed, and commented happily that he was suffering from Natal fever.

'What's that?' I asked, edging away in the hope of avoiding it.

'Extreme lassitude,' he grinned. 'It causes you to sit beneath the Tree of Idleness.'

Then he stared at the river for a socially inappropriate length of time, stretched luxuriously and said: 'It seems to me that today fishing will be inevitable. Wanna come?'

Where the wild things are

The spotted hyena plodded down the road with hunch-shouldered intent. He was going somewhere important and the lights of the vehicle were not about to deter him. When we got too close, though, he remembered something in the grass beside the road which needed checking. He climbed the bank, his short back legs seeming to tuck under his shoulders as he went and lay down.

He was pretending not to notice us, of course, but our presence made him lose concentration and he failed to see the nest between his paws. The sudden rustle under his nose caused him to leap backwards and land on his haunches, shock clearly written all over his face. The striped mouse squeaked angrily, then (not wanting to push its luck) dived back into its grass tunnels. The hyena, all dignity lost, skulked over the bank in a way that only a hyena can skulk.

We were on a night drive beyond Mpila Camp in the heart of the Umfolozi section of the Hluhluwe-Umfolozi Park, spotlights probing the dark and flooding sudden gaps in the acacia woodland. It was a fruitful expedition, yielding cervals, impalas, white rhinos, more impalas, some giraffe, buffaloes, even more impalas....

When we returned to Mpila an entire lawn behind the bungalows was carpeted with impalas, which all seemed to have comfortable expressions of ownership. In terms of numbers they certainly do predominate. There are some 23,000 in the Hluhluwe-Umfolozi Park and each one is as cute as a cuddle-toy. They're such an archetypal antelope, with elegantly curved horns on the rams and very doe-like expressions on the ewes; all with Bambi eyes and little flippy tails.

But now in the autumn rutting season the rams were bucks with business. They herded their harems all over the veld, scooting after stragglers with leaps and bounds and four-point turns.

If another ram so much as raised his head in the vicinity, the suitor huffed and hissed, then did what can only be described as a lion impersonation. The result wasn't quite lion – it was somewhere between pig, baboon and the sound of a cheap can opener addressing a tin of peas – but coming from an antelope it is startling. If you didn't know what it was you'd expect something far bigger and more threatening than an extra from the *Lion King*. The opponent generally got the message, and if he didn't, a jab with a sharp pair of horns was sure to make a deeper impression.

'I just love this place,' sighed trainee ranger Steve Hulley the next morning. 'Will you *look* at those colours?' He swung his arm across a hillside of combretum woodland greeting autumn in shades of green, orange and yellow. 'When I arrived here it was as though I'd come home. Now I never want to leave. This is … this is … so *Africa*.'

Together with Hluhluwe, Umfolozi is the one of the two oldest game reserves in South Africa, having being declared in 1895. That it has survived the combined onslaughts of hunting, poison spraying and modern agriculture is nothing short of a miracle. The area has been inhabited by humans for around a million years and in the previous century it became the site of Shaka's 'great hunts': game was driven into large pits between the Black and White Umfolozi rivers and speared by his warriors. However, by comparison with white hunters and then farmers, the effect of these hunts had little negative impact on the rich wildlife of the area.

After Shaka's death in 1828 European hunters began to deplete the great herds: by 1890 the last elephant in the area was shot; by 1900 the last lion. Before the turn of the century trophy hunters had reduced the Southern African population of white rhino to about 100. Although the reserve was declared a protected area, the killing didn't stop. In 1918 cattle farmers were given land near Umfolozi and they blamed wild animals – particularly buffalo, antelope and zebra – for the cattle blood disease ngana, spread by tsetse fly. The first

eradication campaign in 1929 saw more than 27,000 head of game shot. Then in the 1940s some 70,000 wild animals were destroyed and the spraying of DDT by aircraft began. The slaughter ceased only when the reserve passed into the hands of the Natal Parks Board in 1952.

Rhino were spared outright culling during this period – their hides were considered too thick to be of interest to tsetse flies – but by then they had been reduced to a handful anyway. The story of their rescue from what seemed certain extinction is synonymous with the park's history and earned the Parks Board an international reputation as a conservation agency. Today Hluhluwe-Umfolozi is home to about 2000 of the great creatures: the largest herd of southern white rhino in the world. At the centre of a park now showing no signs of this tormented history is Mpila Camp, perched atop a ridge of hills with the same name. Rather appropriately, camp manager Doug Parrott and his wife Lil (who runs the shop) collect carved rhinos.

'I had a lot more,' said Doug sadly as we waited for Lil's tea and scones. 'They were on a shelf that looked as if it needed support and I asked a chap to do it. He left them there as he worked and they all crashed to the floor when the shelf suddenly tilted.'

His compensation, though, is that rhino and buffalo wallow in the water-filled scrape at the edge of his terrace and hyena test their teeth on a pole outside his bedroom window.

Mpila is an unfenced camp and signs warn you to stay inside after nightfall when predators prowl. In my hurry to make it to a game walk one morning I rocketed out of my chalet's back door and fell over the back of a zebra mowing the lawn.

'The little herd's taken up residence in the camp,' confirmed Doug. 'But it does attract leopards and lions.'

There's an old-fashioned simplicity about the camp, which has two seven-bed cottages, six five-bed chalets and 12 huts which share a kitchen. A self-guided walk up a hill beside the camp (with appropriate signs warning that you should avoid being eaten) offers magnificent views of the hills and valleys between Mpila and the Black Mfolozi.

The sense of being unfenced characterises the camp and the entire reserve. More than half of Umfolozi is a wilderness area where access is restricted to people on foot or horseback. This is land set aside and managed, according to the Parks Board, 'in such a manner that its pristine character is not altered in any way'. No permanent structures are allowed and nothing taken into the area may be left there.

It was here that the concept of wilderness trailing was introduced to South Africa in 1959, and gained momentum as a result of one of the reserve's key conservators, Dr Ian Player. (Another champion of the idea was Nick Steele, who died in 2002.)

To trail and overnight in this area is to feel the ancient heartbeat of the continent. Buffaloes eyeball you as you walk, rhinos graze peacefully, seemingly unconcerned at your passing, lions watch you at night and hyenas investigate the perimeter of your camp site. The undoubted stars of Umfolozi, of course, are the big mammals. In three days I saw almost everything large except the big cats. But in the wilderness area a leopard saw-growled its way round our camp in the darkness and lions in the area frequently roared into the night.

On my last afternoon at Mpila, perched above the meandering Black Mfolozi, I glanced to one side and found I was in the presence of a huge nyala bull. He seemed all built for battle – his heavy body and muscular legs were only prevented from looking like an armoured car by the quirky Mohican hair job down his back.

His neck was immensely powerful and it certainly needed to be – such horns must have sent trophy hunters of old wild with excitement. They curved upwards, then in and up again, ending in lethal white tips which had that polished look of well-used tools.

The whole battle image was completely thrown, however, by the softest of eyes and what looked like a pair of pince-nez glasses perched between them. When he lifted his head from grazing, the nyala gave the distinct impression of having just looked up from reading the *Bush Tick Times*, or whatever would interest a nyala.

As I held its questioning but unafraid gaze, a hyena whoop-hooped and a baboon grumbled lazily along the cliff edge. A sense of peace seemed to sigh through the woodland and a little inner voice enquired: 'Why be anywhere else?' Ranger Steve Hulley was right: Umfolozi is so Africa.

A world apart in the Great Karoo

'I love Somerset East,' said Albert van der Walt, his arms wide and his voice booming amid the ageing printing equipment. 'I love the old people, the young people, the white people, the brown people. I love their arguments, their sadness, their fun. This is my town and, man, it's just perfect.'

By then I'd been there for four days and it seemed a reasonable thing for someone in Somerset East to say. Several weeks earlier, however, I'd had to go hunting in the index of a map book to find the object of Albert's love. There it was, a dot between Cookhouse and Pearston on the R63. Next to it was a small red star and the words 'Historic Buildings'.

Albert's newspaper, *Somerset Budget & Pearston Advocate*, should have a brass plaque reading 'Historic Cultural Object' at the front door. There aren't many country newspapers like that any more. Three generations of Van der Walts have used woodblock, hot metal, litho and now computers to keep the townsfolk supplied with what Albert describes as 'a letter from home'.

The day I was there the headline was about a tree blown down in a thunderstorm and there was a photograph of a puffadder beaten to death and found to have 40 babies inside. The war in Baghdad didn't warrant a mention.

::

Out of Graaff-Reinet, the road to Somerset East was so flat it made me feel a bit weird: no matter how fast I drove nothing changed. Then, quite suddenly, the black ribbon of tar wound into the charming Plains of Camdeboo with their mesa mountains. Round a sweeping curve and there was the Bosberg, a dark brow of forested mountain above Somerset East.

The berg looms large in the history of the town. In 1771 a wagon trundled up to its skirts under the whip of Willem Prinsloo, who dug in and never left. Some years later the Cape Government set up a farm there to supply troops. It was run by a Scot, Robert Hart. When it was proclaimed a town, Hart moved to a valley nearby and started a farm named Glen Avon, which his descendants have never left.

The English explorer William Burchell rode into the area by chance in the early 19th century and was captivated by the teeming life in the Bosberg. He hung around for a month, collecting and sketching. It's that sort of place: difficult to locate, then hard to leave.

When the town was laid out in 1825, the *Government Gazette* advertised it as 'one of peculiar beauty which possesses unparalleled advantages'. As I rolled down the main street, staring at wonderful old buildings framed by the towering mountain, it seemed a fair description. While many of the little Karoo towns I'd passed through on the way seemed to be unravelling, Somerset East had the feel of a busy tapestry still very much in thread.

Somerset House confirmed that. Once a school and more recently an industrial storage space, it has been lovingly restored by Vega and Stephen van Niekerk into a guesthouse that rivals any in Southern Africa. Vega's meals are the sort you'd expect in only top-class city restaurants, and from the deep back stoep, across a wide lawn, rises that mountain.

Before my suitcase had hit the floor Vega was organising adventures. 'Paulet Street is full of wonderful old houses to photograph. And the museum is just great. Go talk to Emile Badenhorst who runs it. They've also got a Walter Battiss collection. You know he was born here? Old Ma Dora's grave is also in the grounds; she lived to well over 100.

'You must also talk to Sheilah van Aardt, she knows the whole history of this town. Oh, and this afternoon we're going fly-fishing in the Mountain Dam with Kevin and Kerry McCaughey, they run the pharmacy. You want to climb the Bosberg? Really? It's high! Maybe Emile will go with you, he runs the hiking club. Or I can get hold of Tina Engelbrecht, she's a great hiker.

'Pity you've missed the Biltong Festival. If you hang around long enough, though, you can run the Bruintjieshoogte Marathon.'

Talk about small-town networks. I was soon whizzing round drinking coffee, eating sweet-cakes and being introduced to life beneath the Bosberg. We did go fishing, way up on the mountain and until after dark. Emile's museum was chock-a-block with small-town history (the best kind of history), Sheilah van Aardt duly arrived with scrapbooks going back several hundred years and later I stood, thoughtfully, beside Dora's grave in a shady bower wondering what it would be like to remember the Anglo-Boer War from the vantage point of the 21st century. And Vega was correct: Paulet Street is extremely photogenic.

On a Monday afternoon I drove out to the fields of Gill College to watch cricket. It's a fine old school, which started life as a little university. Under the trees I was surprised to find a crowd of parents, with cool boxes of food and drinks, cheering on their lads. Now I ask you, where else would you find parents camping out on a Monday afternoon to watch their children play cricket?

After a lazy lunch at Jacques Restaurant, which also seemed to double as the midday pub, I bade Vega farewell and took the road out to Glen Avon, Robert Hart's original farm. Its owners, Alison and Bill Brown, are his direct descendants, the sixth generation to farm there.

Glen Avon is nestled in a beautiful valley skirting the ever-present Bosberg, a few kilometres from town. It's a Thomas Hardy sort of farm, with a working overshot water mill, a house with metre-thick walls, yellowwood beams and a deep stoep overlooking Alison's luxurious garden – complete with geese and sheep dog. We took a wild ride up a deep gorge to stand beneath the Glen Avon Falls. Baboons barked at the unaccustomed presence.

'How high is it?' I asked Alison.

'Not too sure,' she answered. 'But once a cow fell off the top of the cliff and when it hit the bottom it just exploded. Bits everywhere.'

Well, maybe farmers have unusual ways of measuring things.

That evening we sat on the stoep sipping Bill's home-brew (he has a cellar full of the stuff) and I remembered something Albert van der Walt had said. 'This *dorp*, it's not Colesberg, it's not Noupoort, it's not Aberdeen, it's not Graaff-Reinet nor Cradock. We've got trees. It's green. We've got fountains, we've got water. It's not just klip *koppetjies* and dust. I'll never leave.'

I couldn't fault that. After another few home-brews I made a firm resolve to see the estate agent on the way out. We're still negotiating.

In Settler country

Diagonally across from the Pig 'n Whistle are some steps leading down to the front door of the Corner Shop, Bathurst's answer to a supermarket. After a session at the Pig one night, Uncle Doug Dold reversed his Oldsmobile across the road in preparation for an assault of the steep hill leading out of town.

His judgement being somewhat impaired, he overshot the reverse and hung his back wheels over the steps. The fellows in the pub heard the Olds revving wildly and went to investigate. There was Uncle Doug, fixed expression on his face, foot on the accelerator, gunning the now-useless back wheels. One chap strolled over and asked what was up.

'Get off the fucking running board,' Uncle Doug yelled back. 'You'll fall off and break your fucking neck when we go round the corner at the top of the hill!'

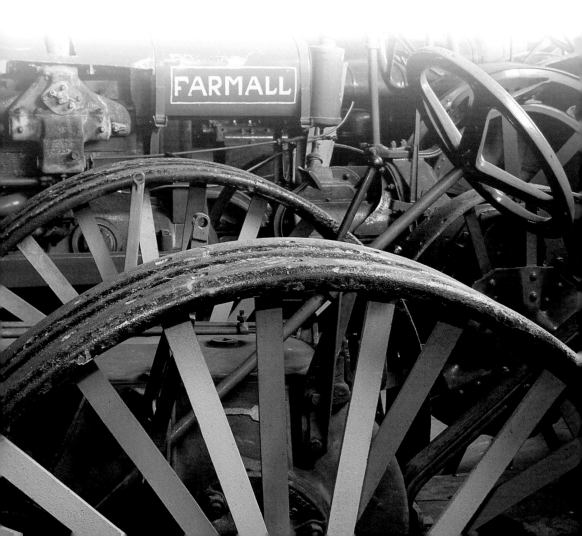

The story was being related by pineapple farmer Alan Pike who was, just then, using his smart Mercedes like a 4x4 on a rough road to an eyrie high above the Kowie River at Waters Meeting. It was worth the ride in both views and stories. Alan's also patron of the Bathurst Agricultural Museum – and he's of 1820 Settler stock. There's something about settlers. They're the ones who didn't stay at home, took a chance on life and gathered skills like snowballs on a slope.

Take Rob Gess. He's a palaeontologist, market gardener and manufacturer of herbal ointments. A useful settler indeed. Anna Wolf has built two yachts; the last one she welded herself up behind the Pig. When the winds are right she'll sail away – to Madagascar, or maybe St Helena, she isn't sure.

Barry Hartley, whom I met in the pub, is a forester, sometime blacksmith, sometime botanist and woodcarver who makes beautiful sneezewood spoons and candlesticks. The Pig's restaurant is named Widow Hartley's – there's a connection. Michael Sheehy – Irish of course – is an engineer and sometime urban planner who's planted a maze in his back garden on the pattern of the one at Hampton Court. Pat Burnett invites faeries into her garden at Tir na Nog and sells them. I'm not kidding. She also sells healing herbs. Sue Willers runs Bleak House, which deals in settler ghosts, coffee and fine cheesecake.

I could go on like this for pages. You don't get these sorts of people in the city. If you ask the 'boets' and 'swaers' in Lower Albany to explain such multi-tasking, they'd shrug and say: 'settler folk'.

Some have been there for generations, related to the priests, parishioners and farmhands who, ruined by the English Enclosures Act, sailed south to the Cape Frontier in 1820. Others are refugees from crowded cities, people who stopped over one day, looked around at the green trees, commonage and rolling hills and said 'yes!' and moved in. Settlers all.

I booked into the Pig – though there are plenty of B&Bs – and was treated to the sort of meal you don't expect at a small country hotel. All I can say is, when in Bathurst, do not fail to order Cyndi Louw's duck and cherry pie. And the seafood lunch platter includes dangerously delicious prawns and fresh East Coast oysters.

Cyndi and her husband, Michael (better known as Mickey Louw, former Springbok show-jumping captain), bought the hotel and have been renovating its reputation and table ever since. The Pig has the oldest pub in South Africa and is obviously the centre of the village. And there's proof: whenever Bathurst's dogs can't find their owners, they generally try the pub first. As a result, the place has a continuous stream of local mutts.

Bathurst is saturated in history. There's St John's Anglican Church (the oldest unaltered church in the country), a school and houses dating to the 1820s, Bradshaw's Mill (where the first cloth was woven from wool in South Africa), the beautiful little Wesleyan Chapel and, of course, the Pig itself, which has given shelter to governors, lords and scoundrels for nearly 200 years.

I finally managed to tear myself away from Bathurst and headed for Salem in a rather fancy Porsche I'd borrowed – not quite an 1820 oxwagon – picking my way past worried dogs.

Salem's the sort of village you'd miss if you blink. The only person I saw was the shopkeeper, who was, at the time, taking a cow to pieces behind the counter. On a blackboard were chalked the prices of choice cuts.

A bit up the hill perched the delightful old Salem Methodist Church peeping from behind tall cypress trees. It has been many things: a school, a fortress against Xhosa attacks and the witness to happy weddings, squalling baptisms and long sermons. David Livingstone's wife, Mary, was schooled there, as was Theophilius Shepstone, once governor of Natal Colony.

The Salem Valley was settled in 1820 by Hezekiah Sephton and his party of 344. The real hero of the time, however, was Richard Gush. When Xhosa warriors raided the area and drove off the settlers' cattle, he shamed the chief for his behaviour (the chief apologised) and offered his warriors bread and tobacco as well. After that, Salem was left in peace.

There didn't seem to be anywhere to stay in Salem, so I scooted up the road to Assegai Lodge, on the N2 some 30 kilometres west of Grahamstown. What an extraordinary country seat it is.

The original farm was built in 1717, and later the British used it as a military garrison. Dick King of the famous ride was based there for a while, as was his horse, Somerset. When the garrison relocated, the buildings were re-invented as Assegai Lodge, a popular wagon stopover between Port Elizabeth and Grahamstown. The lodge has been refurbished way beyond its former glory by Savvas and Amanda Koushis, and today it is an utterly beautiful haven of peace and good food. If you need a bit of excitement you can peer through the shooting slats and imagine a war or two.

I left by Porsche, not by oxwagon, followed by two dogs, probably looking for their master. What is it with settler dogs?

The Island

Patrick Matanjana's eyes were so sad it was difficult to look into them. 'Twenty years in B-section,' he was saying. 'When I came back to be a tour host I was shocked by the walls. When you're a prisoner you never look at the walls – it would make you go crazy. But now: these little cells, these terrible courtyards....'

There can be few places on the world's tourist map which harbour such painful contradictions as Robben Island – and such surprises. In a conversation a few weeks after South Africa's newest tourist destination opened to the public, Patrick and Avril Brand were finding out about each other. Both wore the distinctive Afro shirts of 'Island' tour hosts, but Patrick had served nearly half his life in a cell for uMkhonto weSizwe activities and Avril was the wife of the last prison governor.

'You used to burn your newspapers in the dump,' said Patrick. 'But, you know, if you lie papers flat they don't burn in the middle. So we'd smuggle them in afterwards and read them. They were central to our education programme.'

'You're serious?' asked Avril, startled. 'We didn't realise … well, I think it was a good thing. I'm glad you got them.'

'And we never saw your village or the mountain,' continued the ex-prisoner.

'But I was never allowed into your prison,' said the warder's wife. 'It's all different now, hey?' she laughed.

The island, South Africa's own version of Alcatraz, is an enigma wrapped in a contra-diction, and its new tenants are still exploring its oddities and each other (six of the new tour hosts are former political prisoners and three are former prison department warders). Just past the beautiful Victorian guesthouse (then empty) is a rusty car with the words 'WELCOME ALL BLACKS' painted on the bonnet. The only clue that the irony was not intended was the date of the Kiwi rugby tour underneath. Beyond it – at a street sign declaring the houseless, dusty track to be Residence Road – is a breathtaking sight: Table Mountain as few have ever seen it from land.

'When I bring people here it's not worth telling them anything,' says Avril. 'They never listen, they just stare.'

A little further along the coast, when I was there, bontebok grazed near an abrupt concrete pillar known as Dead Centre. It was used during the Second World War to aim the giant navy guns (which never fired a shot in anger). Few in Cape Town could have realised that, given the position of the guns, if somebody's finger had slipped on the trigger Cape Town's City Hall could have disappeared.

From this point wrecks dot the coastline – the Taiwanese trawler called *Fung Chu 2,* which ran aground in 1977 with 70 tons of tuna on board; a yacht which looks intact from the starboard side but has a hole you could drive a Kombi through on the port side; a whale jawbone arched upwards like the arms of a ghostly dancer. Near the stone quarry where many common-law prisoners were crushed to death in rock falls over the years is a foghorn called Baby Maker (warders claimed it woke them up, and there was nothing to do but cuddle). Penguins shuffle and mutter below the rusted shell of a machine-gun nest.

The island's village is no more coherent and seems uncentred and empty. The Trust Bank is housed in the old leper morgue and is reputed to be the smallest bank in South Africa. Sir Herbert Baker's beautiful Church of the Good Shepherd, also built for the lepers, has been deconsecrated, stripped and stands empty. The Anglican church (which used to raise a pink flag when a girl was born on the island or blue for a boy) stands white and proud a little further down the road like marzipan on a wedding cake.

Across the road is the house which was built for Dr William Ross, director of the leper colony (located on the island from 1846 to 1931). One can only speculate about what took place in the dungeons recently found underneath. Beside the tiny post office is a monolith with ancient inscriptions on its side – it's thought to be the site of the original post stone where, from long before Van Riebeeck's time, messages were left for passing ships. Nearby, houses where warders lived (with burglar bars) stand empty.

Occasionally weather-beaten cars roar past like props from *Mad Max*, their silencers long disintegrated. One has holes where its doors rusted out, another uses a piece of fishing line as an accelerator – it dangles from a gap where the radio used to be. Many are abandoned hulks, used only as a moorage for grass seeds and play-pens for the island's many rabbits. According to tour host Dierdré Prins, there used to be only three traffic rules on the island: cars require at least one head and tail light, reasonable brakes and a windscreen wiper in front of the driver.

Inland is a maze of tracks. One leads to the lighthouse on Minto Hill, the spot where fires were lit as beacons for sailing ships, another to the leper graveyard. Still another runs straight across the island through the alien forest and, at the time of my visit, provided a convenient race track for a pair of ostriches.

Then, of course, there's the terrible lime quarry where Nelson Mandela and other 'politicals' dug in the dazzling white heat, the prison itself, the bleak yard in B-Section and that now famous tiny cell where Mandela spent 18 years (the inhumanity of that detention only dawns on you fully when you see its minute size and remember the breadth of his spirit).

If all this sounds disjointed it's because Robben Island is, and seems always to have been, at odds with itself, and a metaphor for a country out of step with the rest of the world. This is reflected in the very elements which constitute it. But the island's enigma has become a worldwide drawcard. Since opening it's been packing in the tourists.

The natural environment is, if anything, even odder than the cultural one. When Bartolomeu Dias reached the Cape in 1488, Robben Island consisted of low scrub and was inhabited by thousands of seals and jackass penguins. Over the centuries the seals were exterminated – the Dutch and the English clubbed them for their oil and skins, the Scandinavians preferred them served baked in prunes and honey.

English crews considered the penguins to be 'feathered fish'– the island was once known as Penguin Island. In the words of one sailor, the birds were 'so naturallie simple that you may drive them as you would do a flock of sheep' up boards and into waiting boats for slaughter.

Today the penguins are back, but in much-reduced numbers, and the seals have been replaced by bontebok, springbok, rabbits, ostriches and little white domestic ducks. The trees are almost exclusively alien, as is the Indian chukur partridge, but the black oyster-catchers, sacred ibises, sandpipers, arctic terns and 71 other bird species are not. And below the waves, despite undoubted poaching over the years by warders and others, there's still an abundance of crayfish and perlemoen. It's also the best grandstand you're likely to get for the breathtaking daily moods of Table Mountain.

The peaceful art of chucking back

This small Midlands reserve is about boats. But boats are also about fishing and, looking at the crew pointing poles at the lake, fishing is about being at peace with the world.

This, I decided, had to be the key to Chelmsford, because the barbel and carp they were hauling out of the water hardly seemed worth all the time and equipment invested in their capture. Indeed, the silence around the lake was so profound it made my ears zing.

But, although most visitors put their backs to the land and their faces to the water, the reserve has a lot more to offer than mud fish: grass, for example. It's veld type 66, as ranger Caroline Sanford informed me while we thumped along in her 4x4. Wandering through it are more than 100 oribi as well as red hartebeest, black wildebeest, Burchell's zebra, Cape fox and a slew of rats, mice and shrews. Overhead flit healthy-looking representatives of 210 bird species and a goodly showing of bats. If the silence begins to get oppressive, you can always put your ear to one of the giant mounds of *Macrotermes natalensis* and listen to the scritch of millions of fungus termites doing the bidding of their 100-millimetre queen. Or you can grab a mountain bike and follow a rock bunting.

Not having a rod, or a hook to throw at the water, I did the next best thing – hire a canoe and head west along the bank. From this low vantage Chelmsford Dam is vast – some 3000 hectares in fact – so hugging the bank seemed the safest thing to do. The only problem was the lines in the water. The minimum number of rods per person seemed to be four, each propped up on two supports jabbed into the grassy bank. I pulled in to ask a fisherman about his technique.

'Well, there's barbel.' he informed me. 'You catch them on worms. Mud fish. I don't eat barbel. And there's carp; for that you use pap. That's what I'm going for....'

'What are they like to eat?' I enquired, thinking about porridge.

'Actually I don't like them; they don't taste so good. Fishcakes maybe. I just do this for the peace and quiet.'

All the fishermen I encountered seemed to have got that to a fine art: they all had little floats (called 'policemen') clipped onto the rod-end of their line and had settled down with six-packs. If a fish had the temerity to bite, the float was yanked out of the water and its hunter would amble over and reel it in.

'Got a four-and-a-half-kilo carp last week,' called an ample-waisted fellow as I paddled by, just out of sinker range.

'What did you do with it?' I asked, thinking he probably now had a grateful cat.

'Chucked it back in....'

Further along the bank a father was sizzling up a late breakfast on a skottel, while his young son, who was dressed in what looked like dad's checked shirt, hunched expectantly over a single rod. The two had clearly overnighted on the bank and the silent communion between them was wonderful to see. Fishing wasn't the real issue here, I sensed, just a catalyst for something finer.

That evening Chelmsford Nature Reserve showed it had a few more tricks in its bag than peace: the lake's waters were suddenly lit up by an immense electric sky show. To the rolling applause of thunder, almost continuous bolts of lightning hammered down, up and sideways, turning trees into ghostly flashdancers and leaving jagged black after-images across the shattered sky. The rain fell elsewhere, but staccato heaves of wind cooled the night and grounded the mozzies.

The dam was built in the early 1960s – in a wide basin fed by the Ngagane River – but the reserve was proclaimed only in 1975. It encircles the lake but does not venture far beyond its shoreline and has virtually no indigenous trees. Roosting birds have to be content with isolated stands of black wattle, gum and the occasional oak.

There are eight chalets and some 30 camp sites along the dam's edge. I parked my gear in a chalet, only to discover that they also attract other than discerning human guests. Sitting reading in the slanting rays of the afternoon sun, I became aware of a quick movement just beyond my comfortably outstretched legs. I was, I discovered, being regarded by a beautiful yellow mongoose. Its fox-like face was intent with inquiry and its whiskers quivered in anticipation.

After a few moments I returned to my book and, in a flash, the little creature had stolen a piece of cheese from my unattended sandwich and shot into the nearby undergrowth. Seconds later it was back with two comrades and the trio formed a silent picket line just beyond my boots. Cheese, it seemed, would be just fine for supper.

::

My quota of perfect peace was found, not at the end of a fishing rod, but beside Potter's Cottage at around sunset. It's a rough little shack amid tall gum and oak, away from the road and right at the water's edge.

Beer in hand, with my back against a towering gum, I watched Namaqua doves and a pair of fish eagles come in to roost. In the west another storm flashed and rumbled, swallowing the sun and painting the lake and distant shore in shades of blue and purple.

A flight feather from one of the preening eagles whirligigged down onto the grass at my feet and swung like a weather vane. Rain tonight, sunny tomorrow. Peace, it seemed, is derived from simple things. It's just a case of being in the right place at the right time. If I had a rod just then I'd have reeled in the sunset – and not thrown it back.

The village that reinvented itself

The village had vanished, though I could judge its position by the screeching of egotistic roosters. Overhead a grinning new moon, 384,000 kilometres away, seemed closer than the warm bed I'd vacated half an hour previously to stamp up the hill.

A golden sun gradually disentangled itself from wraiths of mist and frowned hotly on the blanketed valleys all round. The acres of cotton wool below me began to move – grudgingly, then sliding faster and faster to who knows where. The trees appeared first, giant copper beeches planted by Dutch settlers more than 100 years ago, then the steeple of the Dutch Reformed Church. For a few minutes I could see my shadow against the mist below and I jumped around a bit to make it do something, hoping that nobody was watching, and yelled, 'Good morning, Dullstroom!'

It's an unfortunate name, conjuring up images of a comatose Mpumalanga dorp and hoary locals with little to do beyond watching the bar counter warp. When Dutchman Wolterus Dull founded it in 1884 it probably was all those things. Three years later it consisted of 48 souls, eight houses, three stables, ten cattle kraals and the Boeren Handelsvereniging shop. You can imagine.

It's certainly not like that now, and the reason for its rise to prominence depends on whom you talk to. There are several versions. One has to do with a Falkirk Union Seven coal oven and eight cream scones at the Rose Cottage Tea Garden.

According to this version there was Nothing of Consequence in Dullstroom until Anita Minnaar bought an old, run-down, corrugated-iron house on the road through town and set up the tea garden (and the stove).

Locals thought it a bit odd because who stops at Dullstroom to drink tea? But people did. On the first day the teashop made R18 and Anita got really excited about that. The rest is history. When I popped into Rose Cottage, people from all over the world were consuming tea, scones and giant sticky things known as *Tant Sis se koeksisters*.

Another version involves a clock, a hole in the wall and a million rands. Remember the *Sunday Times* Finder's Keepers competition in the 1980s? You had to follow the extremely cryptic clues each week to discover where the loot was stashed. A woman from KwaZulu-Natal tracked it down to a cemented-over hole behind a clock in the Dullstroom Inn. The publicity that generated, say some, put the village on the map.

The third and most enduring version has to do with fish, and the honours are divided between a hotel and a shop, though they could also include a watchmaker and a stationmaster. The watchmaker was 'a stocky little German from the Black Forest' who, apparently, stamped around the hills of Lydenburg in the 1920s and '30s carrying trout fingerlings in a petrol can, releasing a few in every stream he could.

Another possible candidate was the stationmaster responsible for delivering a batch of fingerlings to a farmer near Waterval-Boven. The fish arrived in bad shape and he was advised to dump them. He did, in a local river, and they flourished.

At some point corporate Johannesburg discovered the joys of throwing flies at trout-filled dams, and syndicates bought large areas around Dullstroom as private pieces of neo-Scotland. Then in 1988 Howard and Ingrid Walker, who'd bought some ground in the village, opened the doors of Critchley Hackle, a country-style lodge built round a dam stocked with trout. You no longer had to be corporate to catch speckled fish, and urban fly-fishers soon found their way to this highland country retreat. When I visited it, the trout were so big the bobbing ducks seemed to be at risk.

But let's not forget the shop, for it is indeed memorable and pre-dates any of the other claimants on Dullstroom's fortunes. Known as The Blue Shop, it was started in 1916 by 'Rooibaard' Vaid, and it's now fair to say the place is one of the best-known fly-fishing tackle shops in the world. There is a story, probably true, about a Johannesburger who, some years ago, visited the House of Hardy in London (the Harrods of fly-fishers) and said to the salesman behind the counter: 'I come from South Africa, the land of Gary Player and Chris Barnard.' To which the salesman replied: 'I'm sorry, sir, I'm not familiar with those names. But in your country I do know Mr Vaid of Dullstroom, who is the largest purveyor of Hardy equipment in the southern hemisphere.'

It really is a blue shop, and is run by Yousuf Vaid and his son, Mahmood, both of whom are expert fly-fishermen and happy to spend time imparting their skills and local knowledge about snagging trout. 'It's never a problem to help people,' chuckled Yousuf, who was reading the Koran and fasting when I popped in to sample his wares. 'The time spent fishing is not subtracted from a man's allotted lifespan.'

Every item in the shop has a marked price and then there's a 'bargain price', which is arrived at in the age-old tradition. It's dangerous to enter if you find gadgets irresistible, and the variety can be judged from the selection of flies available: at last count more than 50,000. People don't visit The Blue Shop from Gauteng only, they come from all over the world.

Whatever the reason for the popularity of the village, the result begins building up each Friday evening in the form of shiny vehicles with 'GP' number plates. By Saturday it's a deluge: Dullstroom has about 300 permanent residents and up to 2000 visitors each weekend. At around 2000 metres above sea level, they come to cool off in sub-alpine temperatures and fish in mist-blanketed streams and the municipal dam.

To keep them happy there are 16 pubs and eateries, but the favourite is probably still the old Dullstroom Inn. Its pub has a seemingly eternal fire going in a wide brick hearth, dark-varnished pine ceilings, brass plates, wine barrels, pictures of fish and some beautiful photographs of Scottish country life.

One of the wine barrels has a plaque which reads:

'Guinness Book of Records
Vernon Kruger remained in a barrel on top of a pole
for 67 days and 14 minutes
between 17 March and 23 May 1997 at Dullstroom.'

On the other side of the pub, a picture of a Labrador on the wall has the inscription:

'Wake to Sam
His fart was worse than his fight
RIP.'

The inn is owned by Nigel and Sue Briggs and it offers accommodation, good food and the cosiness you'd expect from a family hotel with a long and interesting history.

It was from the inn's warm bed that I braved the misty mountain, but the name 'Die Tonteldoos Bistro' lured me into the village for breakfast. It served an excellent full English (or was it Scottish?) breakfast, though the dinner menu on the wall was exotically provincial French. From its glassed-in porch I watched Dullstroom getting into gear for the day.

From this vantage point, the most impressive sight was the dressed-stone Old Transvaal Inn, owned by Leonard Bert. When I bumped into him over a cup of coffee later that morning he was planning The Dullstroom Gathering. By all accounts it was to be a busy affair, with a fishing competition, Anglo-Boer War event, a music festival, sheep shearing, an off-road biathlon and pole chopping among much more. The date? Well, the town was still working on it.

Hanging around Gia Bert's sweet shop in the Transvaal Inn, I picked up a bit of gossip worth repeating. A rift, it seems, was looming between village citizens because of a flag. Someone had run up a Union Jack over an Anglo-Boer War grave just outside town. But overnight someone else had pulled it down and replaced it with a pair of his underpants. Clearly, old battles take more than 100 years to settle.

A visit to the railway station was a bit disappointing. It's the highest in South Africa, but it looked as though it had altitude sickness and a bad case of peeling paint. Talking about height, Die Berg nearby is the highest point in what used to be the Transvaal.

The post office was more down-to-earth, but also in the 'biggest, highest, first' bracket: the clerk informed me proudly it was the only GPO in South Africa with an open hearth. Now there's a distinction!

It was Monday and the Gauteng crowds were back at work. Dullstroom basked in the mild morning sunlight and the only activity seemed to be around the bank.

Around lunch time I began asking advice on the best place to grab a meal, but opinions differed. The Vaids of The Blue Shop recommended Brian's Plate, Liesel Labuschagne at Dullstroom Accommodation insisted it was Tonteldoos Bistro and I also had a standing invitation to eat at the Dullstroom Inn. Then I remembered someone commenting that real Dullstroomers could be found at The Poacher. Outside the pub a youngster sat beside a battered bakkie filled with scrap iron, looking rather forlorn: his pa was having a drink and he wasn't allowed inside. I ducked through the door and pulled up a bar stool. Men in blue overalls with oily hands were making black marks on their beer tankards.

Manager, chef and temporary barman Lawrence Stucke slid a glass of Windhoek Lager across to me and McCallen the bar cat – named after a single malt whisky – leapt onto the counter, plopped down and stared at me insolently over the top of my glass. Lunch was not what you'd expect in a pub: feta agnolotti pasta with garlic mushrooms, well-stuffed spinach and smoked pepper trout rounded off with apple-and-rhubarb crumble. And another Windhoek. The afternoon, let me be honest, began to blur a little.

Later, sitting round a roaring fire, Scotch in hand, in the Dullstroom Inn pub, I discovered another possible reason for the dorp's rising popularity.

Behind their superficial and largely imagined charm, most South African dorps are pretty boring places. Dullstroom, on the other hand, really is the quaint and friendly sort you imagine dorps ought to be. As the Gautengers roar in and prices rise up to meet them, however, the challenge is going to be how long its residents can keep it that way.

Confucius once said the only constant in life was change itself. But some things just stay better the way they are.

IN DEEP WATER

Going under

Paddling wild

Deep poling the Okavango

Going under

When we die – unless we do it in our sleep or fly a Cessna into a mountain without noticing – I suspect our overriding thought will be: 'This is ridiculous!' That's the thought I was having hanging upside down in a kayak in mid-ocean, unable to pop the skirt. Even dolphins have to come up to breathe occasionally, and the seven-metre kayak attached to my lower body was, right then, preventing me from doing that.

I yanked hard and repeatedly on the release cord to no avail. Then, by accident, I did in panic what inexperience had prevented me from remembering: jacknife my knees. The skirt popped in an explosion of bubbles and I found myself bobbing beside the upturned kayak gasping for air.

'You spent quite a while under there,' said kayak instructor Leon Franken, giving me a hard look.

'Yeah. Great view,' I grumbled, leaning on the point of the kayak to flip it upright.

We'd been doing practice exits off the white-cottage fishing village of Paternoster on the Cape West Coast. This entailed voluntarily rolling into the soul-freezing Atlantic, popping out the kayak, righting it, then clambering back on board. The wetsuits offered little protection, somehow, and the breeze rippling the sea surface and gently lifting the squawking gulls left us teeth-chatteringly cold.

'When we're done here we can go surfing,' Leon coaxed. 'Surfing's great fun. But remember to brace.'

I didn't remember. Bracing means leaning on your paddle while jamming it behind a breaking wave. If you don't, and if you forget to lean into the wave, you roll. In shallow surf that means the heavy kayak slams your face into the sand at speed and you plough the seabed with your jawbone for a while. I write from experience.

My extended dunking reminded me that death was a necessary companion to adventure sport: without it lurking in the shadows there'd be no virtue in delightful acts of madness. Take the skin of a kayak, for instance.

A modern sea kayak is a wonderful craft. You're sealed in, it carries a load sufficient for week-long adventuring, it has a rudder giving it excellent manoeuvrability and it goes like a rocket. However, out at sea, diving over rollers creasing an unreasonably vast ocean, its two-millimetre shell seemed woefully fragile. Okay, so it's made from smart-fibre laminates. But thinking about it elicited much the same feeling as glancing at the window ledge of a Boeing flying at 10,000 metres and noticing the thinness of the plane's skin.

Let's just say that, on that particular day, I was having a tendency to stare into shadows.

Well, building confidence was what we were doing in Paternoster: an advanced course in sea kayaking run by Coastal Kayak Trails under Leon's watchful eye. Those who know the area will understand that the location was half the attraction. Just south of Paternoster is Cape Columbine Nature Reserve, its coastline dotted with huge granite boulders, seal colonies and, in the right season, whales.

Paddling round the great rock domes beneath a china-blue sky upon a turquoise sea is the sort of thing that makes kayaks seem easily affordable extras. And people travel round the world to find places like that. So, from afar, a jawful of sand or a lack of air seems a minor irritation.

It's just that there were a number of questions which, on that day, wouldn't go away, such as how deep was the sea below me and what would happen if a howling southeaster blew us over the horizon?

There was also another question I really should have avoided asking. The sea was kicking up a bit off Columbine, little wavelets going one way and larger swells going another. Every now and then a really big set would come through, lifting the kayaks high enough to see the Columbine lighthouse. We were heading for an isolated pile of ocean-encircled boulders literally cloaked in seals.

The stench was … well, powerful; the sound of roaring bulls spectacular. Beneath our hulls the water was opaque and I got to wondering what might be lurking down there. The wrong question was: 'Do you think there are any sharks around?'

Leon gave me a long-suffering look, maybe considering whether to spare me the news, then answered: 'Yep. Great whites. They feed round seal colonies. Try not to fall out the kayak.'

As we approached the colony, gambolling seals came out to inspect. The sea around us roiled with dark, sinuous bodies. Each one would scoot underwater for a bit, then stick its head up in a good imitation of a car-park bollard and go 'arf'. Multiply that by several hundred, then add the roaring bulls to the growling breakers, and you have an intimation of the bedlam. As we paddled away I hung behind the line of kayaks, marvelling at how human-like a rock full of seals can sound – easy to mistake them for mermaids.

Two dark forms suddenly shot under my kayak, did a wide arc and came barrelling back towards me just beneath the surface. The kayak immediately seemed frail and unsteady. I positioned my paddle to swat them off and wobbled precariously, in danger of tipping myself, I imagined, into the hungry jaws of a pair of great whites. Two sleek, dark heads broke the surface just beyond paddle-swat and said 'arf' in two-part harmony. I nearly swatted them anyway. Still, it was a wake-up call. I paddled down the front of a great green roller and up to my buddies bobbing against the horizon.

Out there at butt level the waves are interesting. There are two types: great, long groundswells, often generated by foul weather thousands of kilometres away, and shorter wind-waves whipped up close by – and often travelling in a different direction.

In the deep ocean beyond kayak range the big swells can reach up to 60 kilometres an hour: great for surfing if you have the stomach for it. Sidling up to land, they slow down, averaging a modest 15 kilometres an hour. In an eggshell boat, though, even that's fast.

It's much easier, but not as thrilling, paddling into swells. This is because when running with them your kayak tends to want to broach (depending on the type of kayak). But when you go, you really go.

The lift soon passes, of course, and you seem to slide down the back end. If you're the nervous type, it's not a good idea to glance over your shoulder just then. A mountain of water from the next swell coming in your direction can be unnerving.

Some earlier paddling lessons reduced the anxiety, though. 'Bend your arms only slightly and rotate your body from the hips,' Leon had advised. 'Keep only the blade in the water and push with your foot on the same side. That way you transfer the paddle power to the kayak.'

We'd sat on the beach, drawing arcs in the sand with our paddles, learning the backward power stroke, the draw stroke, a forward sweep then a back sweep and, in case a wave smacks you on the nose, a back brace. Eskimo rolls? 'Later,' Leon had waved away the question. 'It's better to first learn how not to capsize.'

Next morning there were whales in the bay. In the still air before the southeaster got going we could hear the 'vroosh' of their blowholes. Kayakers in South Africa are allowed to approach to within 300 metres of these great summer migrants and we were keen to try.

We dutifully kept our distance as the mysterious creatures huffed, slurped and lob-tailed just offshore. Why are whales so compelling?

The tail which slid up among the kayaks was a complete surprise. It belonged, I guessed, to a southern right whale and was heading straight for my boat, completely ignoring the 300-metre limit. It must have been 15 centimetres thick at its base and was a good couple of metres and then some out the water. The half-imagined creature from the shadows had emerged – spectacularly.

I sat, spellbound, curiously unafraid, watching black doom approaching, thinking: 'This is ridiculous.' A few metres from my kayak the huge tail slipped under my craft and disappeared. Whales, it seems, have good road sense.

I sat, bobbing in the waves, my ears ringing from the excess of blood my thumping heart had seen fit to deliver. Then I dug my paddles into the sparkling water and powered down a swell, flinging up paddle-scoops of spray and whooping in delight. Maybe death stalks in many guises. But so do angels. And right then, bobbing in a kayak under an airbrushed canopy of sky seemed exactly the right thing to be doing.

Paddling wild

The idea had been irresistible: to kayak Tristan da Cunha, the remotest inhabited island on earth. It had been a good cocktail-party conversation but … why not? So next day I phoned the St Helena shipping line. Would they take kayaks? Sure, they said, no problem.

'You're mad, of course,' insisted Captain David Roberts of RMS *St Helena* when I called him up to confirm. 'The weather down there's unpredictable. It's just off the Roaring Forties and slap in the middle of the South Atlantic. You'll probably die but, well, that's your business.'

So one sunny Cape Town morning saw Neil Rusch and me hoisting sea kayaks over the deck rail of the *St Helena* and stowing them in the ship's cavernous forward hold.

Not many ships sail west from Cape Town into the setting sun. Soon the seagulls fell behind and around us was nothing but empty sea.

The *St Helena* has excellent anti-roll stabilisers but is somehow too short for the long Atlantic troughs. So for five days of total idleness and far too much good food we rocking-horsed our way towards the tiny island. After a while I got used to the motion and, after the trip, found it difficult to sleep in a bed that didn't rock like a cradle.

Tristan slipped into view early one morning, a brooding volcano with near-vertical walls of black lava disappearing into a surprisingly calm sea. It is, indeed, the remotest permanently inhabited island on the planet, St Helena being 1200 nautical miles up the Greenwich meridian and Cape Town 1800 nautical miles to the east.

'You're lucky with the weather,' said Captain Roberts, seeming a little disappointed. Perhaps he missed his Royal Navy days of wild seas when men were men. Having been awed by tales of the island's legendary nine-metre swells, I was delighted.

From its base on the Mid-Atlantic Ridge to its occasionally snow-capped crater, Tristan is around 6000 metres high with some 2060 metres sticking out of the water. Its steep sides provide little space for the village of Edinburgh and near-impossible conditions for a harbour. So the *St Helena* dropped anchor offshore and we were ferried in by friendly, weather-beaten Tristanians. As the Tristanians were fishermen and boat people, the two kayaks attracted a good deal of interest. The locals make beautiful, canvas-covered longboats, but they'd never seen such strange craft as ours before.

'Watcha goin' ta do wif 'em?' a burly fellow enquired.

'Go to sea,' said Neil.

'Naah! You're not serious.' He shook his head worriedly. 'But the weather be good today....'

The kayaks were hauled onto the quay from the longboat ferry, bright splashes of colour amid the oily cranes and fibre-glass fishing boats. Tristan has a nasty reputation for sudden weather changes, so we decided to get our kayaks in the water as soon as possible.

This posed a problem. The little harbour was purpose-built for fishing boats, which are dropped into the water by crane, not run from a slipway. The water was a good metre and a half from the quay top.

There were the remains of an old slipway, but it was broken and kelp-covered, and looked decidedly dangerous. However, a great splodge of the stuff had built up in a corner of the harbour and took my weight when I stepped onto its ooze. I dragged my Skua onto it and seal-dived it into the water, paddling frantically to avoid being chucked back by a surge.

Neil was fussing about somewhere, so I powered out of the harbour before an audience of dozens and into the open water – savouring the idea of being the first kayaker ever to do so in Tristan. After about half an hour – time enough for me to paddle round the *St Helena* – Neil scooted up and we set off westwards along a spectacular coastline.

Tristan comes in three intense colours: night-black lava, emerald-green grass and turquoise sea. The effect is psychedelic. While the top of the volcano was clothed in cloud, the sun lit up the lava platforms littered with vents and the sides of the 600-metre base scarred by deep 'gulches'. Round one corner the rocks fluoresced with slashes of bright-fire orange.

I was staring so hard at the weird island that I didn't see the yellow-nosed albatross until it had nearly scalped me. They're strangely inquisitive birds, completely unafraid of humans, and they were quite prepared to buzz us at close range, skimming the waves. They never seemed to flap.

Another one finally plunked itself onto the water beside us and powered round the kayaks to within paddle distance to see what we were about. Close up we could really appreciate the huge size of these beautiful birds. Wandering albatrosses have up to four-metre wingspans and their yellow-nosed cousins are not much smaller. We paddled past the potato patches and alongside sharp rocky fangs to Anchorstock Point.

'I think we should go right round the island,' Neil said.

'You're nuts,' I protested. 'It's late, this is one damn big island and nobody knows we're going to attempt it.'

Neil sat looking south for a good long time, then reluctantly followed me back towards Edinburgh village.

Back in the harbour, as I beached the kayak, trying to avoid getting dumped face first into the smelly kelp mush, Neil slipped quietly out to sea again. I figured he wanted to take a trip round the St Helena, as I had done earlier, and stowed my Skua beside a rotting yacht which had been dismasted and washed ashore.

When Neil wasn't back by six o'clock that evening I began to worry. When he wasn't back by eight, the island administrator notified the chief inspector, who mobilised a rescue crew. They were preparing to launch two fast boats when, at nine o'clock, the St Helena radioed that they'd spotted Neil coming round Anchorstock Point. He'd made the circumnavigation.

When he arrived, cold, shivering and exhausted, he was treated to a severe dressing-down by the inspector, who said he'd never used his handcuffs before, nor the prison cell, but he had a damn good mind to use 'em right then. The administrator looked stern, the rescue crew were mightily irritated. Neil had broken almost every rule in the kayaking book.

Back on the St Helena as it set sail for Cape Town a few days later, Neil looked a lot less contrite.

'When the fuss blows over, what have I got?' he asked with a wicked gleam.

'A record?' I suggested.

'Yeah, right.'

Deep poling the Okavango

It had all the trappings of a normal expedition: a good plan with an unknown outcome. The idea was to pole the Okavango Delta in dugout canoes from its beginnings at Seronga to where the wandering waters finally died in the desert near Maun. Perhaps 150 kilometres, maybe 300. Nobody knew for sure. Conceived a year earlier between *Getaway* editor David Bristow and Peter Comley of Untamed Africa, it would be the first non-stop traverse of its kind.

Like David Livingstone, I took my wife, Patricia, but unlike him we flew in to Seronga over the swamps in a small Mack Air Cessna. It took a mere 45 minutes from Maun. On a couple of ex-Kariba houseboats – now renamed Okavango Houseboats – we met some of our fellow travellers: Gary Mondale, an inveterate adventurer from Minnesota; Steve Krenzen, who runs the Association of Professional Guides in California; Steve's friend Daryl Browne, who was taking a break from selling cars; Ken and Hillary Owen from Johannesburg (he an engineer and she a deacon); a Washington lawyer, Nanette Paris; and Diane Smith, a New York executive between jobs. Like the membership of any expedition out of Victorian annals, it was a mixed bag if ever there was one.

Next morning, on the papyrus-clad banks of the lower Panhandle, we met the polers, led by 67-year-old Sariqo Sakiya. The old man sat on his folding chair, watching his men store a prodigious amount of gear and people into nine slim mokoro dugouts. Then he climbed into his canoe and headed out through the grass-covered shallows, followed by the rest of us in a flotilla. Within minutes we were pushing through high papyrus. Startled little spiders rained down on my lap and every now and then a drooping sedge, its tousled head in the water, would be whipped up by the mokoro and slap me wetly across the face. By lunch time the truth had dawned on us all: this wasn't going to be a paddle in the park.

::

The Okavango Delta is a beguiling place. In summer, tropical storms rumble and flash across the high Benguela Plateau in central Angola. Water pours off steep slopes, gathering sand, leaching salts from the sodden earth and picking up speed as it gutters down long, straight valleys. By the time it reaches the northern border of Botswana it has become Southern Africa's third-largest river.

Here it channels into the Okavango Panhandle on a wide, meandering journey towards the Gumare Fault, a tectonic extension of the Great Rift Valley of East Africa. It is thought that the Okavango, together with the Chobe and Zambezi, once flowed into a vast lake covering what is now the dry Makgadikgadi Pans.

Geological faulting gradually tilted and lifted the earth's surface, diverting two of the rivers northwards to their present courses and creating a great trough which absorbed the flow of the Okavango. Over time this filled with silt, windswept sand and organic debris, becoming a delta which today looks like the leg and claws of an eagle – or, as Daryl suggested while peering at the map, a great green cannabis leaf.

The Kalahari, a great semi-desert covering most of Botswana, is exceptionally flat: across 250 kilometres of the delta the elevation drops a mere 61 metres. Water which falls in the Angolan highlands in December, and which pours into the Panhandle at a staggering 11 cubic kilometres a year, takes six months to fill the Okavango's furthermost channels and can in good years reach Maun.

Once in the delta, the only way for the sparkling, clear waters to go is up: swallowed each year by the atmosphere through evaporation and plant transpiration. That's 16,000 square kilometres of vanishing water. Out among the islands, the water gets involved in some really complex chemistry.

::

It had seemed a good idea to keep a diary, and the first entry got the scale about right:

'With all these green stems above my head I feel like a mouse. The spiders don't worry me – they're small – but the five-metre crocodiles do. I asked Peter where they live and he said "Oh, in the papyrus." The possibility of giant saurians hungrily eyeing our progress was disturbing.

'We crossed a lagoon covered in lily pads and delicate white flowers with sky-blue centres. Beautiful African jacanas were hopping round, looking for lunch. To distract myself from the crocs I looked up the jacana in Daryl Balfour's *Okavango, an African Paradise*. It seems the female makes the nest, lays the eggs, then goes off whoring and leaves the male with all the housework. He hatches the chicks, cleans the nest of shells, forages for food, carries the young on his back and clasps the chicks under his wings when danger threatens. He's a great dad.'

By the time I'd finished writing that down we were out of the papyrus and it was noon. We needed a break and everyone was wondering if Sariqo had planned lunch stops. He had. We shoved our way through sharp sedges to a wild beach. Lunch was much finer than we'd expected.

'There's some warthog dung up there,' Daryl announced.

'So how would you know?' demanded Gary.

'Hey, I asked my poler. I wouldn't know the difference between warthog droppings and my own.'

Later that afternoon, as the sun dipped, Sariqo began searching for an island on which to camp. There are about 50,000 of them in the delta, but he is a fussy man. The first had a fine Pel's fishing owl, but the grass on the salt-covered centre was wickedly spiky. Finally he approved one with soft grass, a ring of paperbark acacia and spiky fan palms.

An extraordinary amount of gear was disgorged from the mekoro (that's the local term for a gaggle of mokoro) and we soon had a fire going, dome tents, a shower enclosure and, behind a tree, a rather comfortable toilet. In the tradition of Livingstone, before turning in I diligently updated my diary:

'In the strange silence before the orchestra of the night, island palms were silhouetted against a golden sky. The first sounds of the darkening water world were the grunts of waking hippos, then the sweet sounds of a fiery nightjar calling "Good Lord, deliver us."

A fruit bat began the klink, klink, klink of hammer on anvil, and myriad reed frogs seemed to take that as a signal to plink their urgent mating calls.'

That evening Sariqo requested that Hilary say a little prayer while we all stood in a circle. Several days later Peter mentioned that the old man had dreamt that he was lost, and the prayer was an appeal for guidance. Considering the fathomless tangle of green and countless islands, I continued to hope the prayer had been answered.

The next day we packed and left in biting cold. My poler, Babiwans Ketiholwe (he asked me to call him Fox), was a man spare of frame but with a powerful pole action. Standing in the back of the mokoro, he pulsed the canoe along steadily and silently.

Slouched in the front, a few centimetres above the translucent water, with reeds and lily pads sliding by, it occurred to me that the journey could easily shift from idyllic to surreal. The truth is that adventure is seldom adventure when it's happening: it's what you recollect in tranquillity later. What was happening had to do with slipping down sedge-walled slippery paths, spider rain and snorting minibus-sized hippos.

As the temperature rose around noon I erected my camera tripod, and draped a kikoi over it and the seat behind me. It kept the sun off, but all I could see was green stems and, in the distance, date palms, jackalberries, paperbark acacias and the occasional umbrella thorn waving slowly as we slid past endless islands. For hours. And we still had 10 days or so to go.

That night a lion roared nearby, an elephant walked into camp and Gary turned into a pyromaniac, stacking the fire into the sort of blaze which made coals in which you could forge iron. It is a little unsettling to discover that, in paradise, you are mere food.

::

The rhythms of the delta weave life and death together with ever-changing complexity. Unlike most rivers, the Okavango carries very little mud, salts and nutrients. Most of the sediment is sand. Because the river has no outlet, salt is accumulating at the rate of about 450,000 tonnes a year. This should have killed the delta ages ago, but it hasn't. The reason is that swamp trees quarantine it.

Papyrus and hippo grass dominate the channels of the upper swamp, allowing water to escape slowly into back-swamp areas but confining the sandy sediment. These back-swamp communities – grasses, sedges and other aquatic species – return the water into the atmosphere by transpiration and produce peat, while bacteria fix dissolved salts. On islands

lower downstream, trees transpire so rapidly they cause the water table beneath the islands to fall below the level of the surrounding swamp. As a result, ground water from beneath flooded areas, where most of the salts congregate, flows under the islands, accumulating in the centre.

Eventually the toxic salts destroy all plants on the island. At this point the floodwaters should erode it and release salts into the swamp. But, with perfect timing, papyrus and hippo grass upstream will have encroached into their channels, causing sand levels to rise and blocking their flow. The water is diverted elsewhere and the old islands dry out.

Then, mysteriously, the peat in these dry areas catches fire, and summer rains flush saline poisons deep below ground. Nutrients from the fires combine with sand to form fertile soils which produce lush grasslands. Because the area is so flat, the loss of peat causes the level of the land to drop, and swamp water gradually reclaims the grasslands. In this way the delta renews itself.

::

About two days deep, my diary entries began to fall apart. As we slipped between lily flowers, a flock of open-billed storks lifted off the water and circled above us, looking strangely like pterodactyls. A fish eagle, patrolling above them, flicked away in seeming irritation. Writing about all this felt strangely detached. It required a point to what we were doing, when there seemed, just then, to be no point other than to watch life passing by. I managed a few more lines:

'I seem to be shedding my urban skin. We have to get to Maun, I guess. But do we? As the waters of the delta beneath us slow across the Kalahari sands, we also seem to be losing mental speed. I'm here doing absolutely nothing, watching bounteous life sliding by, feeling no compulsion except to be. I have just spent a considerable length of time watching a beautiful gold and green beetle (probably yet to be classified) walking slowly up my leg. A line of red lechwe suddenly burst into the open beside us, plunging through the shallows with the sound of breaking waves and throwing spray into the sunlight. I didn't reach for my camera but just sat there, watching.'

The strange inertia worried me, but later, around the campfire, I discovered that others were feeling the same. Our lives, we decided, had slipped into a waking dream of clear waters, green stems and wild creatures.

::

By noon the next day the papyrus had given way to rustling phragmites reeds. The water lilies had changed too, having smaller leaves and delicate yellow petals. The islands, though, were getting bigger, which, Peter said, meant more animals. Gary, sitting in the front of Sariqo's lead mokoro, was the first man round each corner. We all agreed he was perfectly placed as bait. Soon afterwards there was a roar of massively disturbed water and two bull elephants appeared from behind the reeds. They eyeballed us but continued on their way. Gary seemed to crouch lower in his mokoro.

My diary recorded unfocused inertia: 'I could be losing it. I'm not sure which day of the trip this is – the fourth or fifth? The rest of life has disappeared and we are adrift in a water world that seems to go on forever. It is so completely beautiful that, like the withdrawals of a heroin addict, my future normality may prove sadly disappointing. There's just the rhythmic splash of the pole, the lament of a red-eyed dove and the chatter of bulbuls.'

That evening the dream was about to trade places with a nightmare. We pitched our tents under an immense jackalberry on Xhara Island and, as we sat round a fire, the maniacal cackle of hyenas stopped all conversation. Cautious torches picked out yellow eyes all round the camp.

As people edged into their tents a bit later, the eyes moved closer. Of our fire only a small flame remained, casting a soft glow on my tent. As I zipped myself into my sleeping bag, a huge shadow fell across the tent, shoulders hunched higher than a malevolent head with its jaws gaping. The thin skein of logic collapsed into raw fear so ancient and primitive that I gasped. For maybe millions of years such creatures had eaten my ancestors, and every cell in my body knew it.

The spotted hyena passed the glowing log and the shadow vanished, leaving me hyper-ventilating. Later that night there was a crash and a yelp. At dawn we found that one of the cool boxes was missing, the top had been chewed off a vacuum flask and a tub of Bovril was missing. We later found a tin of Milo ripped open and the contents licked clean.

::

We spent two nights on Xhara, giving the polers a rest, then moved on, glad to be rid of hyenas. The following night we camped on a beach on Nxabenga Island. An elephant walked towards us, stopped in surprise, then strolled off into the palms. Round the fire that night the Americans got into intense conversation. Nanette and Diane seemed to be taking strain, but I retired, not wanting to become involved in their angst. We were all being thrown back on ourselves and everyone had their own way of coping with it. That night a strange spirit wind plucked violently at the tents, then was gone, leaving the night calm and clear. In Tswana tradition, it meant the passing of a wizard into the underworld.

We pushed through a continuous mass of reeds for several hours the next day, then drifted across pools of flowers sparkling with countless, multi-coloured dragonflies. My diary became lyrical but brief:

'This is an isolated beauty in no urgent need of beholders. It's an invitation to commit poetry or philosophy or any number of higher or contemplative crimes.'

A large crocodile lunged across our path and hippos snorted explosively, then sank beneath the flowers. Red lechwe seemed to be everywhere. We gave a bull elephant a wide berth, and a large buffalo bull sized us up, thinking evil buffalo thoughts for a moment, then went on his way. Peter was right: as we headed south between larger islands, animals were coming thick and fast.

That evening we pitched camp within Moremi Wildlife Reserve. Back from the water were savanna-like plains sprinkled with warthogs. We sat round the fire, some of us staring at the vast universe above, others fussing over chores.

'The maxim I live by', said Peter suddenly, 'is this: two men in prison look out their bars, one sees mud, the other sees stars.'

'Well, all I see is stars,' said Gary, grinning and staring at his muddy boots.

::

We passed Xaxaba Lodge the next day and gawped at tourists in clean, designer safari gear. To them we must have looked like swamp rats. Later there was a large herd of elephants, which took off at a run, leaving billowing brown dust in their wake.

We camped on Xaga Island that evening, unconcerned now about the whoop of hyenas and the growl of lions. We were becoming attuned to the ways of the delta. Before dawn, as usual, our cook Gassie coaxed the previous night's coals back to life and perched a kettle over them for tea. The previous evening Sariqo had estimated that we might be only three days from Maun. I dug for my watch and discovered from its calendar that we had been travelling for eight days. Was that really possible?

If we held the pace, a record was due to tumble: as far as Peter could establish, it would be the first non-stop mekoro trip from Seronga to Maun.

A further bragging point would be that Peter would be the first white person to pole the whole way in a single journey. This had won him some admiration, and plenty of ragging by fellow polers. He'd done the journey with Gassie perched in the bow.

'Ahiee!' the occasional local we met would exclaim. 'A white man poling a black man. Ho, ho, ho.'

I sat watching the tousle-headed palms composing themselves in the first light of a delta dawn. Then the impact of Sariqo's estimate hit me. Panic – only three days left in paradise!

::

That morning we passed a hippo feeding in the shallows, his great jaws going whump, whump like a John Deere harvester. He was so engrossed he didn't see us coming until we were close, then he gave a threatening snort and plunged into deep water, there to regard our passing with *grrumphs* of steaming breath.

Whirling vultures – lappetfaced, whitebacked and hooded – led us to an island where a large male lion was chewing contentedly on a downed buffalo. We beached and crept up behind a termite mound to within 50 metres of him. He saw us but went on chewing. It suddenly dawned on me that it would have taken several lions to stop a buffalo that size and that his companions were probably just then staring at our unprotected backs. We beat a cautious retreat to the mekoro and cast off.

Sariqo led us into a maze of waterways – channels and backwaters weaving round large and small islands. It was a mystery how, without a map, compass or GPS, he knew where to go. That night we made camp late, having tried to make up distance lost through the many zigzags. The polers were exhausted and we all bedded down early. We were awakened by the usual sounds: the *kwerri-kwetchi* of a crested francolin, the *hrrungh* of a lion, the sounds of a kettle on the fire and the moan of a hyena. 'In three days time,' I thought mournfully, 'we're going to be sitting in an aircraft, aching to be back here.'

There was an icy wind as we pulled out into the channel past a huffy hippo. The lilies had changed again. They now had big round leaves but small white flowers exuding a heady perfume. A few minutes later a cloud of dust led us to a squabble between some lions and hyenas arguing over a kill. Nearby, like Caesar in the Colosseum, a large male lion was watching the performance from under a tree.

::

Around mid-morning we came upon a hippo grazing on the bank. Some of the group nosed in behind a termite mound and crept up for a look. Through the binoculars he was a large, battle-scarred beast and, as I watched, he put his head down and headed for the mound.

He had the most ferocious expression I've ever seen on an animal: slitty eyes and a deep scowl. We hotfooted it back to the mekoro and pulled out. Some of the polers, however, had taken off down the beach, leaving Daryl sitting in the canoe. 'Run!' we yelled, but he seemed to have lost his instinct for self-preservation. He hunched down as the hippo crested the mound, looking dark and absolutely huge. It was grinding its teeth. Daryl was maybe 10 metres from it and he did the only wise thing under the circumstances: he tried to look like baggage. I thought he'd had it, but the hippo rumbled past him into its pool.

My final diary entry was not much more than a squawk. Quoting from Henry David Thoreau's book *Walden*, it read, 'I came to see if I could learn what it had to teach and not, when I came to die, discover that I had not lived. I came to live deep and suck all the marrow out of life.'

::

We made camp for the last night on Thokatshebe Island. When darkness wrapped round us we could see the glow from the lights of Maun. We were, Peter estimated, only a couple of hours from the buffalo fence. The untamed dream was ending. Eleven days earlier I'd been in a houseboat wondering what 300 kilometres in a dugout canoe felt like. Now I knew: it pains your backside and sets your spirits soaring.

Gary built a masterly blaze for the last time and we sat round it rather quietly. Something needed saying and Sariqo rose to the occasion. He said that because it was the first trip of its kind, it would be remembered in the delta for a long time. He thanked his polers and the rest of us for a trip travelled in harmony and good humour. We all drifted off to our sleeping bags, leaving a soft glow of dying embers. Deep in the night a lion roared magnificently, claiming one of the last wildernesses where he was, indeed, still king.

Next morning, as we left, a fish eagle threw back its head and greeted the dawn. An hour later we poled through the buffalo fence and ran the mekoro up onto the beach. Maun was just down a dusty track.

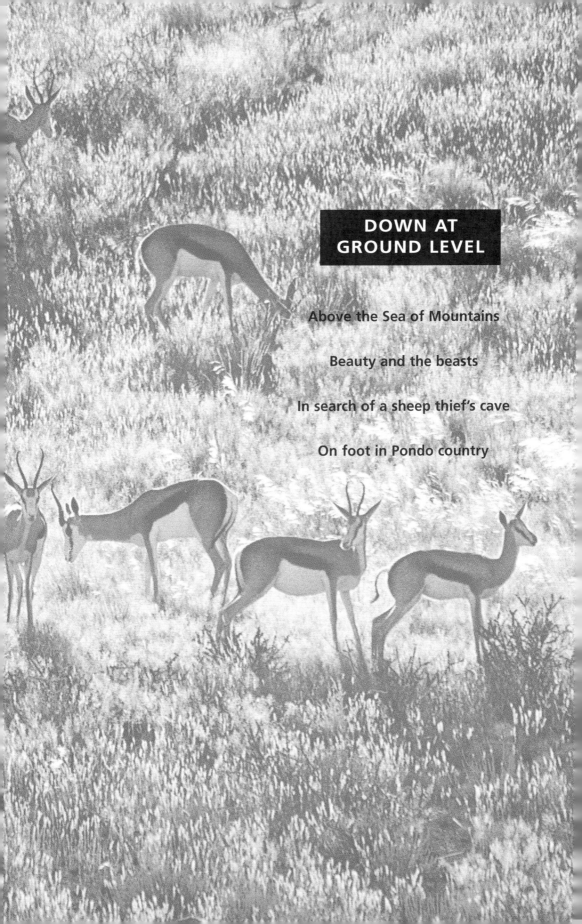

DOWN AT
GROUND LEVEL

Above the Sea of Mountains

Beauty and the beasts

In search of a sheep thief's cave

On foot in Pondo country

Above the Sea of Mountains

My eyes registered the gradient as gentle but, after 35 kilometres at around 3500 metres above sea level, my legs calibrated each step in degrees of pain. The deeply grooved pony track led up through giant lobelia and huge erica trees towards a sky which swirled and rumbled, threatening rain. I found myself chanting my usual mountain mantra: 'Why, why, why do I do this?'

My goal was Imet Gogo (The Mother), a lofty eyrie on the rim of the Great Rift Valley in northwestern Ethiopia – but that was still a long way ahead. Inevitably, it being Ethiopia, two youngsters appeared, seemingly from nowhere. They were dressed in blankets slung, burnous-style, round their bodies and over their heads. One carried some dropping-spattered chicken eggs in a goblet-shaped basket made of tightly woven sisal.

'Eggs?' he said, hopefully. When I failed to respond, the other one tried another tack: 'Hellowhatyournamedoyouhavepenforme?'

'What?' I croaked at him, then realised it was a heavily accented version of a standard local greeting to foreigners. But I was too far gone to be polite: 'Look,' I replied, knowing he wouldn't understand a word I said, 'I've just walked all day through these crazy mountains of yours. Two of my party are back there in that erica forest, suffering from exhaustion and altitude sickness. Now you want me to give you a pen and buy your damn eggs.'

The two looked at me round-eyed, obviously impressed by my speech. Then, simultaneously, they said 'ishee' (cool) and continued dogging my steps up to Gich Camp. It was, I grumbled to myself, one of those situations in which the idea of hiking the Simiens had been too thrilling to allow better judgement to prevail – and now it was too late to pull out.

Earlier that day fellow traveller Neil Lee had done the sensible thing. When a Toyota Land Cruiser had appeared magically at Sankaber he negotiated a price with the driver and slung his pack in the back. His face at the window, as the sturdy vehicle headed back to Gondar, looked both disappointed and relieved. I should have heeded the warning signals back at Debark. In Amharic its name means, appropriately, 'not fair'. It certainly wasn't: it seemed to be filled with the worst sharks I'd ever encountered offering for hire – at hugely inflated prices – dirty camping mattresses, used maps of the Simien Mountains and lifts to Sankaber at costs that would be the envy of Johannesburg's taximen.

We had trudged up through the village's market ahead of the pack-mules, hoping to escape the incessant peddling of kit and services. Apart from some corrugated-iron roofs the place could have been in any century. Hundreds of hopefuls, strewn all about, purveyed rich-coloured cloth, startlingly red peppers, huddled sheep, bolts of bright fabric, Ge'ez bibles, beads and an impossible assortment of junk I couldn't imagine anyone buying.

After hours of slogging through uninspiring peasant fields and dongas, we had pitched camp at Mindigebsa in a downpour. 'It never rains in Ethiopia in October,' our guide, Bedassa Jote, had insisted, looking offended as he coaxed a flame out of the Primus while a drenched mule-minder held an umbrella over him. He soon produced strong, hot tea followed by pasta and a fresh tomato-and-garlic sauce which we gobbled thankfully before retiring to bed at 19h30.

::

The trip to Sankaber the next day was peasant-picturesque but hadn't felt like we were in a national park: it was a non-stop tableau of Old Testament, robed people riding donkeys, shepherding sheep or ploughing steep hillsides with tiny oxen and primitive ploughs.

The Simiens had made themselves felt at the Lamma River, where the path led up and up to a higher plateau. Sankaber had been nothing to write home about – a few huts and a wall-less roof for visitors to shelter under. From here a road had swept us three remaining travellers plus guide, loaded mules, mule-minders and an AK47-toting warden down into a natural meadow which formed the head of a yawning valley offering tantalising glimpses of the Great Rift Valley.

But at that altitude the day's hike had been too taxing for us. Anita Arnot and Ann Griffoen had sat down suddenly somewhere on an endless slope and I guessed the trouble to be altitude sickness: I hoped it wasn't something worse. All that was left of our party was me and my aching legs – and now my companions were two crazy kids trying to sell eggs. If someone got really ill or injured, help was a long way off.

The mules had gone ahead to Gich Camp, the last overnight stop before Imet Gogo, and the little blue tents, when they appeared over a rise, were as welcome as the Addis Hilton. Two mules were quickly dispatched to save the weary hikers and, after a rehydration process and a mug of whisky, the insanity of being here subsided a little. A bright Venus dragged the Milky Way into view, the fire made our sodden boots steam and rice alfresco with roasted maize appeared. In the distance a Simien wolf yipped.

'Not bad,' I thought, but my mind refused to entirely justify being perched on a flea-infested saddle blanket 3500 metres above sea level. This was big, wild, hard country and we weren't at the top yet.

::

Next morning our party was reduced to two plus guide, muleteer and warder; Ann having opted to spend the day at Gich Camp. Anita wisely commandeered a horse and attendant peasant and set off for Imet Gogo in style. The trail led up through forests of giant lobelias with strange flowers soaring up to five metres above their aloe-like leaves.

After about an hour and a half of steady uphill our peripheral views seemed to narrow – as they sometimes do on high mountains. As we walked out onto Imet Gogo's rocky shoulder the trail vanished into nothingness and silence. To the south a massive gorge, with sheer cliff walls higher than Table Mountain, sliced our promontory from the next finger, on which we could see the tiny huts of Chennek Camp. In the gorge waterfalls plunged like silent lace, funnelling water into a tracery of streams and rivers two kilometres below us.

Further south, another finger probed the abyss: Bwahit, at 4430 metres the second-highest peak in the Simiens. Beyond it loomed Ras Dejen, 4543 metres and the fifth-highest peak in Africa. Clouds hovered protectively above it and glaciers drew a white line beneath its crown. Below us, to the east and north as far as the eye could see, was Dip Bahir Wereda, the Sea of Mountains.

I sat down suddenly, tears welling in my eyes, such was the raw beauty which lay just beyond my boots. The empty silence was broken by the hiss of wind over feathers and a huge lammergeyer, catching an updraft, wooshed metres above our heads. It was so close I could see its golden eyes and the subtle adjustments of its primary feathers. Far below a rare walia ibex with massive horns hugged the base of a precipitous cliff. I found myself chanting my other mountain mantra: 'Yes, yes, yes ....'

::

In this area some 40 million years ago great cracks in the continent's crystalline bedrock allowed the basaltic lava beneath to ooze up and spread over an area covering nearly a million square kilometres and, in the Ethiopian Highlands, reaching a height of more than 5000 metres. About 20 million years later, Africa's crust parted, forming the Great Rift Valley – a 6400-kilometre-long rift stretching from Mozambique to Jordan in the Middle East.

As the Rift Valley opened up, the lava cap was literally torn down the middle. Glaciers, then water, ground and furrowed the crack ever wider, separating the Simien and Bale mountains, forming the yawning chasm stretching away before me and creating some of the most spectacular highland topography in Africa.

I plodded back down from Imet Gogo in a triumphal procession consisting of several hundred gelada 'lion monkeys'. These large, bewhiskered primates – also known as bleeding-heart baboons because of a red, heart-shaped piece of exposed skin on their chests – were communicating in sounds so close to human speech it was eerie. They were unafraid of us or our horse as they foraged and chatted, merely turning their backs on us to indicate displeasure if we approached them too closely. The males of this species, once widespread throughout Africa, really do look like lions and, when they bare their teeth, are a fearsome sight.

The two-day return trip to Debark was exhilarating – our legs had been toned by the upward trip, our lungs acclimatised to the altitude and the trail was mostly downhill. Also, somehow, we noticed more going downhill – possibly because the landscape is below the level of our gaze and not above it.

The mountain flora was strangely familiar: it's basically giant fynbos. Evidently, many of the plants which now constitute the Cape Floral Kingdom began in these highlands and, over millions of years, migrated down the Rift Valley mountains and the Drakensberg chain until they could go no further south. As good travellers should, they reduced their bulk along the way, but in the Simiens, forests of erica trees jostle with giant geraniums and everlastings. St John's wort (*Hypericum*) also started out from the Ethiopian Highlands but only got as far south as Mpumalanga, where its common name is curry bush. There were few birds at these altitudes, but the valleys rang with the deep-throated 'ha de haa' of the endemic wattled ibis – this species has a gravelly call which makes hadedas (which are also found in Ethiopia) sound like hysterical schoolgirls. And whenever we ate we were seldom without an attendant cluster of thick-billed ravens. They thumped down heavily, almost within arm's reach, their huge, wicked-looking beaks keeping us on the alert.

As we descended, peasant cultivation brought a marked change to the scenery. It was difficult to believe that people starved in Ethiopia. All about were fields of tef, a grain used to make *injera*, a kind of pancake and the country's staple food. Between them were tracts of wheat and beans. Rivers flowed strongly down the many valleys and plunged thunderously over waterfalls. Although the east and northeast of the country is dry and infertile, the bounty around us seemed capable of feeding the nation for years. I'd hazard a guess that two things prevented this: there are no roads to get the produce out, and peasants, who constitute most of the population, are notoriously difficult people from whom to extract a surplus.

As we tramped down the road out of the mountains a beautiful little girl with tight braids fell into step with me. I estimated her age at about six. She looked up at me shyly, her large eyes twinkling above the fold of her cloak, and began the standard greeting: 'Hellowhatyournamehaveyougotpenforme?'

I dug in the bottom of my camera bag and produced an old Bic. She clutched it with both hands and gave a little hop-skip of delight.

'Ishee, ishee....'

'Yeah, sure, ishee.'

'Birr' (money)?

We were definitely back on the road to Debark....

Beauty and the beasts

There are dragons in the Cedarberg. Manticores glower from the high peaks, chenoo hurl gnarled trees, boggarts bustle below cliff walls, trolls grizzle quietly over their goblin hordes and dark doppelgängers flicker at the edge of your sight.

If you don't already know about these creatures it's because satyrs weave spells of forgetfulness around hikers and foresters who traverse these wild Cape mountains.

No matter: the secret's out. As I pen these lines, my back safely to the wall of a hut below Shadow Peak and the Sphinx, a 30-metre-high cave lion set to watch us has been distracted by a rabbit with 20-metre ears crouched on the valley floor and my notebook has gone unnoticed.

Six hours ago we forded a stream with boots slung over our shoulders and not-yet-smelly socks firmly in hand. Up ahead (and standing nearly two kilometres high) was Tafelberg and a path connecting to a trail running from Pakhuis Pass to a teapot of stupendous size called The Spout, then on to places with unlikely names such as Square Tower Peak, Skalieband, Groot Hartseerkloof and Valley of the Red Gods.

Down there, already, our packs were heavy; but the sharp spring air and a good breakfast at a Cape Nature Conservation hut called Uitkyk near Algeria conservation office had fortified our spirits.

The trail led up into a kloof which must have once been clothed in ancient cedars, but now only a few gnarled specimens with attitude clung to boulders and cliff faces like stranded octopuses with shaggy tops.

Cedars are an endangered hardwood today, but in the nineteenth century they were appreciated more as poles and planks. In 1883 alone more than 7000 cedar saplings were felled to become poles for the telegraph line between Calvinia and Piketberg. Already, at that stage, heavy deforestation over the preceding 100 years had brought the species to the brink of extinction.

::

Gargoyles loomed threateningly as we approached the Welbedacht Cave for lunch. But the hiss of the Gaz stove and the smell of Earl Grey tea kept them at bay as we munched cheese, salami and tomato rolls and struggled to see ancient, faded Bushman paintings along the wall of an overhang which had been blackened by generations of camp fires.

Just beyond the cave the path turned left along a wide and welcome shale ledge known as Die Trap. It seemed to offer an easy stroll round the treeless Sederhoutkop and Langberg to the Sleepad Hut. But appearances are deceptive in these mountains and the jeep track continued wickedly uphill below the snow-capped Shadow Peak.

The way was pocked by a series of small, rocky-edged valleys which once must have been havens for more conventional wildlife but now sheltered mineral creatures frozen in sandstone, seemingly for eternity.

The rocks in these parts have had a tough time since they were deposited as beach sand and estuarine sludge in a shallow Gondwanaland bay some 250 million years ago. Over the top of them came the more fertile Bokkeveld Shales – clayey deposits of huge, linear lagoons – followed in turn by sterile sea sands of the Witteberg Group.

Then, as the super-continent of Gondwanaland fractured, these sandstone and shale layers were squeezed into tectonic ripples and pushed up out of the sea where wind, water and temperature sliced off the Witteberg and Bokkeveld layers and did some serious damage to the Table Mountain Sandstone underneath.

In some places the folds arched six kilometres vertically into the sky before being ground down to size. The result, for good reason, is called the Cape Folded Mountains.

The savage spirit of the Ordovician and Jurassic periods clearly became trapped in the slumbering sandstone because – when time and water sculpted the rocky landscape – frightening creatures began to emerge and to glower upon the puny human hikers who'd supplanted them.

::

We strode on, unconcerned but not unaffected by this wild geological history. The trail eventually curved to the right and down, offering up a rudimentary hut perched on an infinity of valleys and purpling mountains. From here the doughty little footpath enquired of our need to press on to Sneeuberg, Crystal Pool or Die Gat. But we declined, dropped our packs, eased off our boots and sank down in the long grass in the lee of a little cliff with a view.

As the sun sank and was swallowed by the world's edge we busied ourselves with supper, noses down and drowsily pigging, then jerked to attention as the moonless night sky opened with a palpable hiss of stars.

'Look, a scorpion: it's chased the sun away,' said One Who Understood. In the sky, its claws on the western horizon and its tail in the Milky Way, was an arachnid of vast proportions. To its left some visual prodding disclosed a winged horse and a parsec-sized serpent you wouldn't want to tangle with. Suddenly the heavens seemed to fill with eagles, bears, hunting dogs, sea monsters, lizards, unicorns and countless star creatures strung among some 100 billion galaxies – and between *them* the yawning great depths of forever....

It doesn't do to drink too much whisky at the away end of a hike in the Cedarberg: it can give rise to some disconcerting notions about time, space and the scale of your life.

::

Next morning we'd recovered enough to scrape together breakfast and to think about the long way down. Die Trap wasn't so bad this way round and the deep silence was broken by nothing but the squelch of boots in mud and the rustle of ericas in the light breeze.

In Welbedacht Kloof stone sentinels consented with the cedars to let us pass but, as we evened out onto what geologists call the depositional apron, wind satyrs plucked at our memories and scoffed at notions of mountain presences.

In my pocket, though, were notes I can no longer vouch for. But their validity was confirmed by the condition of our cars: in the dust of their bonnets and hoods were strange footprints, and a contemptuous turd balanced dextrously on a rear-view mirror. Some said it was baboons, but others knew better.

In search of a sheep thief's cave

He was probably self-trained, but as a trail guide Kasper was without peer. He met us as we drove into Silwerfontein Farm and inspected our packets and their contents minutely as we distributed loads into packs.

Then, when he was sure the party was ready, he shot off through the gum plantation at the base of our destination, Ontongskop, to check his route markers and trotted back to encourage us on that awful first kilometre that dogs all hikers on this trail.

As the path turned left towards the looming mountainside he located a spring where we could replenish our water bottles, then started up the trail ahead of the party, checking for snakes and other things that worry city folk.

Some 200 years ago a sheep thief named Jakob Ontong claimed this mountain as his own. On Sunday mornings, when the villagers were dutifully in church, he is said to have skulked down into the valleys and snatched his woolly prizes, fleeing back to a deep cave hidden near the summit. His hideout – nearly a kilometre above us in the Voëlvlei Mountains of the Western Cape – was our destination.

Spring is a good time to be in these mountains. There were still patches of snow on the Witsenberge across the valley, but the day was comfortably cool and king proteas were bobbing in the light breeze all round as we climbed a spur to gain the shallow kloof. All about, the fynbos looked the way fynbos should – shoulder-high, sharp-edged and flashing some outrageous colours.

For those who like to know these things, the Voëlvlei and Elandskloof mountains are home to 29 types of protea – including the bashful mountain roses and six Red Data Book species including *Sorocephalus imbricatus*, which grows only in these mountains – as well as 18 types of erica, which all seemed to be in bloom and ringing their tiny bell-like flowers in the breeze.

At about 600 metres above the lake, Kasper called a halt below a cool overhang. High above, a fish eagle screeched and we took this as a signal for tuna rolls and the usual hodgepodge which tastes wonderful on hikes but which you'd never think of combining at home. As our trail guide carried no supplies of his own he gratefully accepted a tuna, avocado and chocolate roll with some water.

Far below, the giant Voëlvlei Dam shimmered silver, and small craft could be seen with lines overboard, their crews (no doubt) with similar intentions to the fish eagle overhead. The dam, with its massive earth-fill walls on either side, was built in the 1960s on the site of a vlei to supply water to Cape Town. Its name is derived from the Dutch word Vogelvalleij, and refers to the abundance of waterfowl found in the valley. Today it's fed by canals from no less than 24 rivers which come out of the Winterhoek Mountains north of Tulbagh.

The proximity of water, forest and mountain habitats has assured the area of a splendid array of bird species – 205 have been listed, including three types of ibis, greater and lesser flamingos, steppe and jackal buzzards, six types of eagle (including black and martial), four types of swifts and four types of swallows, a confusion of canaries, weavers and cisticolas and both greater and lesser honeyguides.

But *our* guide began getting impatient – perhaps because he was a country-raised barefoot type and his feet didn't hurt – so we set off again for the peak.

::

The cave, when Kasper showed us where it was hidden, was spectacular and it was easy to see why a sheep thief would choose it. The entrance was obscured from view by a tree; but from its mouth, amid the seemingly endless wheatfields, could be seen Hermon to the west, the outskirts of Tulbagh to the north and, to the south, the approach to Wellington.

No problem spotting sheep from up there....

The outer chamber of Ontong's Cave is about 15 metres deep, but if you're prepared to leopard-crawl through a hole there's another cavern deeper in, which must have seen many cubs being born before humans came along. The outer chamber roof is at least three metres high, the floor is sand and after six hours of climbing it looked like home.

Sitting high up on a spur of rock we watched, transfixed, as the sun sank through shades of orange and red to leave a shimmering band of liquid light across the Swartland. Then, as we turned around, a full moon rose over the Witsenberge. In the clear atmosphere it shimmered like liquid silver and we could clearly identify the waterless seas of Mare Imbrium and Sinus Roris as well as the jewel-like ray crater with its bright streaks of rock, ejected on impact from an enormous meteorite.

As darkness fell (and the friendly sandstone metamorphosed into sharp-fanged gargoyles) we lit a circle of candles in the cave. It was transformed into a glittering banqueting hall for a medieval-style supper which appeared from within backpacks and which was shared out according the ancient fellowship of travellers.

Kasper accepted our food but spurned the comfort of mats and sleeping bags, choosing instead to curl up at the entrance of the cave to keep watch over us. But the following morning, at first light, he gave a sharp but not unfriendly 'get up' command; and when that was ignored he pounced on a few select sleepers. Those who still slumbered on he ignored for the rest of the day: it was beneath his dignity to communicate with late risers on this mountain.

::

Breakfast was a laggardly affair; nobody wanted to heft packs onto sore shoulders or cram tired feet into the waiting mouths of sweat-stained boots. But, slowly, the line re-assembled and began following the trail of iron standards with orange-sacking markers which indicated the way down.

From Ontong's Cave the path heads northwards along the high ridge of the Voëlvlei Mountains, connecting to a jeep track which winds through a breathtaking wild garden of proteas and shocking-pink ericas.

About 200 metres along this track Kasper led us away to the left into a series of shallow valleys surrounded by fantastic rock formations, all of which seemed to end in sudden wide views over the Land van Waveren, a vast valley wherein Tulbagh and Wolseley and the Witsenberge are found. Far below, the little villages kept appearing and disappearing, and careful binocular work located the Michell's Pass to Ceres.

A slight confusion over orange-bag markers necessitated a quick conference in a field of *skaamrosies*, but our guide was once again decisive and we turned westwards, now bringing Tulbagh into view, nestled in the palm of the Groot Winterhoek Mountains.

From this point the going was down and tough – we tightened our laces to stop our toes jamming into the front of our boots. As the path tilted steeply, Voëlvlei Dam reappeared and the hamlet of Riebeek West, just below Kasteelberg, seemed to hover over endless yellow wheatfields.

Here the orange bags were replaced by rock cairns and there was no water around. But, just when we were starting to imagine Saharan camel trains from the salt mines of Ayr, a cool stream appeared at the bottom of a kloof. Surrounded by buchu bushes, it was the perfect place for lunch.

From the stream the route goes dry all the way to Bernd and Karin Müller's swimming pool at the trail's end on Silwerfontein Farm. Zigzagging through giant protea bushes, the path has the temerity to go up when the soul cries out for down. It was here that Kasper came across a huge porcupine, and carefully kept it at bay until we'd passed by.

Finally, though, there were the lawns of the Müllers' exquisite Cape Dutch homestead, iced orange juice and the deep blue pool awaiting our arrival. At this point Kasper finally took his leave and dived into his owner's fish pond where he lay, grinning a sheep-dog grin and wagging his tail.

When trailing with a guide of his calibre you're in good paws. But remember to take along a tin of first-grade dog food and some extra water.

On foot in Pondo country

'It's the Pondos,' said my father as our ageing Citroën wheezed and boiled its way into the village of Bizana. 'Dangerous people.'

It struck me that they must be very dangerous indeed, given the number of troops, Saracen armoured cars and snarling Harvard aircraft swarming about the place. A few days later I puzzled over a newspaper photo of a row of stately, blanketed men on horseback with spears in their hands. The headline read 'Pondo Uprising'.

Because few white South Africans in the 1960s seemed to know what was going on around them, I never got a clear answer about what caused the uprising. During school holidays in Port Edward or Port St Johns, though, I would gaze at the hut-speckled hills of Pondoland and wonder what savagery was brewing over there.

As I crossed the Mzamba River and hiked along a footprint-free beach beside our guide, Chris Mbuthuma – a Pondo of stately bearing and gentle demeanour – I was reminded of those times. With us were two Cape Town friends, Paul and Pam Nichols, whom I had lured along. Being 61, Chris remembered the uprising. 'So, what was it all about?' I asked as we headed down the coast into the heart of Pondoland.

'Land,' he replied. 'The chiefs tried to give our land to the whites so we had to kill the chiefs … and a few headmen as well. You never take land from a Pondo!'

This reputation pre-dated the 1960s. In the Frontier Wars, British troops stayed well away from Pondoland, and its people were the last Africans to come under Cape colonial administration. Apartheid South Africa, too, left Pondoland chronically undeveloped but also virtually uncolonised. Today it is still thinly populated peasant farming country with few roads, no phone or power lines – and one of the most beautiful coastlines in all Africa.

Were the Pondos dangerous? We were about to find out. I'd discovered that a community-owned tour operator, Amadiba Adventures, ran hiking and horse trails along the coast between Port Edward and the Mkambati Nature Reserve. From there an outfit named PondoCrop was assisting local communities in extending the trail further south to Port St Johns as part of a European Union-funded tourism development programme. It required more than 100 kilometres of backroading, but it was definitely time to unlock the mystery of those hut-speckled hills.

::

Across the Mzamba everything was tangibly different, especially since we'd left Western civilisation by way of the Wild Coast Sun golf course. In place of the ecologically destroyed KwaZulu-Natal coastline and flying golf balls were grassy hills which rolled away from the shoreline like flowing wizard cloaks. The air smelled, not of petrol fumes, but of seaspray, cowpats and woodsmoke. Wearing a watch became about as useful as using a fork to spoon soup. Up ahead was simply daytime and night-time.

The only other humans we came across that day – around lunch time – were a pod of riders going north. Their steeds were loaned from local owners and organised by Amadiba Adventures. The horses all had interesting, pared-down endurance saddles and were in good condition. The Pondos are horse people.

After about 12 kilometres of beach trekking we headed inland to Kwanyana Camp. It consisted of a collection of dome tents and an ingenious water heater that produced several steaming showers on half a cup of paraffin. Several cheerful local women were soon cooking up a fine chicken stew with potatoes, samp, beans and delicious vetkoek. Sated, we then wandered off to visit a cat-like sangoma, Nolitha Ndovela, who danced and stamped herself into a rather frightening trance in order to chat to her dead ancestors.

Next morning, after fried eggs, home-baked bread and maize porridge, we wound our way up into strange red dunes littered with Late Stone Age tools and scarred by the tracks of a bulldozer used to prospect for titanium. The contrast between the pristine coastal bush and the brutal scarring across the rich cultural treasure trove was disturbing.

As we trailed further down the coast Chris entertained us with tales of a fearsome creature named *Inkuyamba* which, he said, lived in lakes and rivers along that coast. It evidently had

great wings and a horse-like head – and ate cows and people indiscriminately. When it moved about, storms and howling winds accompanied its passage. I went 'Yeah, sure' and assigned the beast to the mental company of dragons and jabberwocks. We threaded our way past the mouth of the Sikombe River with its beautiful lagoon and eventually dropped our packs at Amadiba's cosy Mtentu River Bush Camp. It was the end of the 'Rolls-Royce' section of the trail.

The river is the northern boundary of the Mkambati Nature Reserve, possibly one of the remotest reserves in South Africa. Mtentu Camp had canoes, so it wasn't long before we were paddling upriver past spectacular sandstone cliffs to the cries of fish eagles and the querulous peeping of hornbills.

About three kilometres inland a huge black cloud swallowed the sun and a violent wind nearly snatched our canoes off the river surface, sucking up little waterspouts and wrenching at our paddles. Hornbills fled in panic. *Impundulu*, without a doubt. We struggled back through waves which smashed over the nose of the canoes, blinding us with spray, and finally staggered ashore at Mtentu, sodden, but to the comfort of a hot shower and supper.

That night the wind howled, ripping at the tent stays and sucking the canvas into cannon-shot cracks. It was like being inside an artificial, panting lung. Next morning I emerged from my tent bleary-eyed and a believer. Chris was up, hands cupped round a hot mug of tea. I nodded knowingly at him, pointed at the sky and said: '*Impundulu!*' He looked at me as a father would regard an ignorant youngster and said: 'No. It's a July wind.'

Mkambati Reserve has an odd history. It began, in 1922, as a leper colony. When a cure for the disease was found, it became a tuberculosis hospital, then a private hunting ground and, finally, a provincial game reserve. The place is glorious, and the heart of an internationally listed hot spot of plant diversity.

The area boasts at least 130 endemics, including the Pondoland ghost bush, Pondo bushman's tea and the Pondo palm, which grows only on the northern banks of the Msikaba and Mtentu rivers. It's an interesting mix of forests and grassland plus, oddly, plants of the Cape Floral Kingdom.

The government, backed by some contract-hungry corporations, plan to extend the N2 highway through the reserve or along its western boundary and right up the Pondoland coast. If they do, it won't be long before that pristine coastline looks like the urban mess of the KwaZulu-Natal South Coast. We tracked past prowling ground hornbills, across the waving grasslands and through strange swamp forests, trying not to think about the consequences of the road.

Lunch time came upon us at a stream that stepped its way to the beach through pools formed by a series of sandstone ledges – the final drop being a cascade right onto the beach. It was beautiful beyond words.

::

The reserve accommodation – a flat attached to the reception – was adequate though in need of a touch-up, but nearby was a gracious stone lodge which was also for hire.

At Mkambati, Chris headed back home and was replaced by the effervescent Faith Zathelela and three porters who would join us on the second – wildest – section of the hike. Leaving the reserve across the Msikaba River (which, at 35 metres, has the deepest estuary in South Africa), we headed into country characterised by quartzitic tablelands and deep, cliff-lined gorges.

Along this section the hiking distances are longer, the countryside is even more spectacular, and hikers are accommodated in huts with Pondo families. We simply placed ourselves in the hands of our guides, and they were great. Born in the area, they knew the land, the people and local stories.

Faith led us to Port Grosvenor, where generations of treasure seekers have been picking through the remains of the ship of the same name which sank in 1782. Then, beside a deliciously lonely stream, she introduced us to her grandmother, herbalist Eunice Setunsa, who gave us tea and biscuits in her immaculate home filled with crockery and ornaments of a bygone age.

We overnighted in a comfortable hut with a newly dung-covered floor in Rhole village. There we were spoiled rotten with tea, home-baked bread and a country meal of beef, potato-like *ndombes*, stir-fried cabbage and the staple samp and beans. Sponge mattresses with clean bedding were laid out on grass mats, and a bath of hot water appeared on cue. As we watched the sun sink a sled, pulled by four beautifully coloured oxen, bumped past. A delicious peacefulness settled all about. The only sound was the creak of the departing contraption and the distant rumble of waves. How did we ever come to live in cities?

Next day we hit the trail at 07h00. It was to be the longest leg – perhaps 20 kilometres – through some muscular country. The area is undergirded by hard sandstone which meets the sea in massive cliffs and deep, river-cut gorges. At Mkweni River we avoided the gorge and slipped along the beach, wading through the stream. At Luphuthana – a tiny holiday hamlet – the whole area shook with the detonation of huge waves crashing against water-pitted sandstone ledges.

We peered over an edge, then fled as a roaring wave sent great fans of spray high into the air above our heads. At the next gorge there was no chance of slipping past at beach level. It's named Waterfall Bluff for good reason: the river plunges 100 metres over towering cliffs right into the churning sea. We lunched within sight of the falling river, then bid farewell to Faith and her porters – guide Isaac Mlotywa and his team had arrived from Mbotyi. We packed up and tracked inland to where we could cross the Mlambomkulu – the waterfall river.

From there it was hard going across great shoulders of thick buffalo grass and through delightful, human-absent streams until we finally dropped down to the long, curving wing of Shelly Beach, over a headland and into the luxury of Mbotyi River Lodge. There's nothing quite like a hot shower and a beer when you feel you've earned it the hard way.

Mbotyi is a family lodge and was filled to bursting with families. The lawns rang with the laughter of delighted children. It was a hard place to leave next morning, but Port St Johns and the end of the trail beckoned.

There are some spectacular forests along this section of the coast and a few large estuaries. At one point I was up to my armpits in flowing water, at another point high on a cliff watching dolphins surfing the waves far below. Port St Johns, when we arrived, was a rather tatty village wedged between the Mzimvubu River, two high headlands and the endlessly grumbling sea. From there we caught a lift to Umngazi River Bungalows where, with a bottle of red, we held a final Wild Coast banquet.

I need to report, though, that my father was quite wrong. If you're not after their land, the Pondos are among the sweetest, most engaging people I know. But, sadly, he's no longer around for me to tell him so.

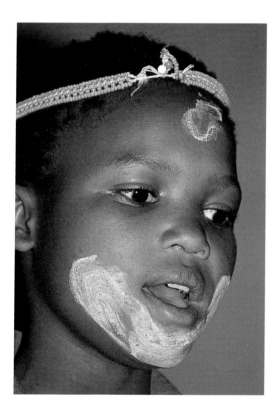

Biking the 29th

Two wheels on the road to nowhere

The bouncing bike, the lonely Russian
and the baby grand

Cycles in the forest

In the hills of Nongqawuse

Biking the 29th

There are times when destination is unimportant, when travelling is its own reward and movement becomes an end in itself. Old Agus Rots, the *karretjiemens* we came across near Grootdrink, seemed worn near to dust from too much moving as he plodded the empty roads with his ragged donkey cart.

In Richards Bay, at the end of the long ride, we found a beautiful singer named Tracy in a bar. We asked her to play 'Yellow Brick Road' for us, but instead she played Chris Rea's 'Road to Hell'. Perhaps it was a warning....

Certainly the road seemed endless – from coast to coast along the 29th line of latitude through South Africa's vast interior. But, astride powerful motorcycles with the wind roaring past our helmets, the towns and hamlets became mere interludes along an alluring black ribbon which urged us ever onward.

Photo by David Bristow

It began in Port Nolloth. The main road out of town heads east and is as straight as a map line. On either side is nothing but tussocky flat sand edged by faraway hills; Springbok lies straight ahead.

My BMW 1100 RT was going so fast it would probably be an offence to even publish the speed, and I found myself chuckling over a story about diamonds which Grazia de Beer had told me earlier that morning.

She has a little guesthouse called Bedrock, but used to run an eatery called Mama's Italian Trattoria. One day the waitress rushed in, yelling that two strangers from up north were beating up her boyfriend outside the chemist. Grazia spied the unfortunate fellow tied, spreadeagled, in the back of a bakkie, which drove off at speed.

It seems the victim had committed the greatest crime of this frontier town – he'd stolen someone's diamonds by swallowing them. The angry pair wanted them back. They went into the chemist for a purgative, but couldn't speak any language the assistant knew, so, from their frantic actions, he presumed Immodium was required. It turned the boyfriend's innards to concrete.

The police were notified and found all three out in the dunes, waiting for the reluctant diamonds to emerge. They were all arrested and the last Grazia saw of the boyfriend, by then fed with a stiff purgative, was in a hospital bed surrounded by policemen also waiting for the diamonds to appear.

That's Port Nolloth talk, which is always about diamonds and usually about IDB (illicit diamond buying). We'd spent the previous evening in the cosy Pirate's Cove restaurant trying to guess who the smugglers were.

The adventure had actually started back in Cape Town in that casual way adventures often do: 'Why don't we bike the 29th parallel?'

'Why the 29th?'

'Well, because it's the widest part of South Africa.'

Somehow the fact that the line went through Springbok and Pofadder settled the matter. A few months later – on a bitingly cold midwinter day – David Bristow, Stirling Kotze and I were astride three large, sensual machines with our backs to the icy Atlantic and our faces towards the warm Indian Ocean on the other side of the continent.

With the freezing wind creeping down our necks on the long ride up from Cape Town the whole idea, not to mention the timing, seemed crazy. But as the BMWs snaked up the Anenous Pass towards Steinkopf and Springbok I found myself singing an old favourite of mine from the film *Easy Rider*: 'Get your motor running, back out on the highwaaay, lookin' for adventure, or whatever comes my way....'

This was going to be cool.

The bikes created a minor sensation outside the Springbok Café. 'Juss,' exclaimed a slightly tipsy pavement patroller, 'where are you guys going?'

'Richards Bay.'

'Where's that?'

'Where the sun rises.'

He looked impressed.

Jopie Kotze is a legend in this part of the world, and his Springbok Café is the meeting place for all manner of characters. We found the man behind a counter strategically placed to allow him a view of his café, restaurant, bookshop and gem collection. He was not fazed by our black leathers and helmets and hauled out a bottle of petrol-tasting *mampoer*. 'It'll keep you warm,' he chuckled.

Behind him was a pair of boxing gloves which once belonged to Robey Leibbrandt. Their owner was a boxer in the 1930s who stayed on in Germany after the Olympic games, becoming a fanatical Nazi supporter. He returned, dramatically, by yacht and landed on the Namaqualand coast, making his way to the Transvaal, where he set up sabotage units. He was caught, jailed, and later released, settling in Springbok, still a hero to many. On the wall nearby was a plaque to Jopie from the Namaqualandse Boerjode (Jewish farmers) with thanks. It somehow didn't fit.

'I'm a man in the middle,' shrugged Jopie when I queried his wall display. 'I like history and people like me. And I don't do IDB, I do gemstones. For me the diamond is not a pretty rock.'

The N14 from Springbok to Pofadder was almost dead straight. It passed through treeless and seemingly endless scrub desert, and was both terrifying and awesomely beautiful. Vehicles on the road were so few and far between that drivers waved to each other reassuringly as they passed.

I edged the bike onto the white line and had the strange sensation of being in a space–time warp. Under a dome of blue on a sea of yellow desert, the black ribbon of road ran like a line drawn from my front tyre to infinity. The only imbalance was the telephone poles along the road which, because of the absence of trees, served as supports for large nests of sociable weaver birds or roosts for pale chanting goshawks. This sure was a great big country....

As we neared Pofadder I became aware of a movement behind some low hills on the horizon: a ghost-like figure seemed to be pacing us. I considered the possibility that the hypnotic symmetry was getting to me, when the form seemed to solidify and resolved itself into a gigantic full moon rising over the rim of Namaqualand. Like the star of Bethlehem it led us to the little town of Pofadder. There was room at the inn.

The Pofadder Hotel had doilies everywhere: big, small, square, round. In the winter months, when things are quiet, hotel owner Nella Britz turns one of the lounges into a sewing bee and teaches her staff to embroider.

'They need something, you know,' she commented, 'there's not much going on here between seasons.' Her parrot, Vicegrip, rang his bell in agreement. Even he appears on the doilies, his image picked out in bright thread, and as we set off to the pub to play a game of pool I could almost swear he made the noise of a motor bike. Smart bird.

The road continued out of Pofadder the way it came into it: dead straight. But it was soon relieved by strange dolerite extrusions which looked like giant molehills. They were stark evidence that our continent floats on a liquid magma sea which appears occasionally in millions-of-years-old rock spouts. By the time we picked up signs for Kakamas the limb-warming alcohol of the previous evening was beginning to take its toll, so we swung off the N14 to take a break at Augrabies Falls on the Orange River.

'You are now entering a WARZONE against chaos, crime, laziness and poverty,' a large signboard informed us. We rode on, nonplussed, and ordered tea and plates of chips at the restaurant beside the falls. The river was running at a mere five per cent capacity, but it still plunged with a mighty roar into the gorge. The Bushmen considered the falls to be haunted, and they had a point.

Beyond Kakamas the scenery changed dramatically as the road snaked up through tough-looking hills and past farms watered by the Orange River. I stopped at a roadside stall to buy some dates but I had to ask the assistant where they were: they were so big I hadn't recognised them. I rolled into Upington like a hamster, my cheeks stuffed with their delicious flesh.

In the past, the wooded islands around Upington were strongholds for river pirates, bandits, rustlers, renegades and desperadoes. The infamous Captain Afrikaner had his hide-out there, as did his lieutenant, a Polish forger named Stephanus who had escaped while awaiting execution in Cape Town. The celebrated highwayman, horse thief, rustler and adventurer Scotty Smith also settled in Upington, where he died of Spanish flu in 1919.

All this seemed to have rubbed off on the traffic cops. One pack lay in wait for speedsters just outside town, another ticketed one of the bikes for touching a yellow line beside a parking bay and our faithful Maui camper, trundling along behind us, received another ticket when a parking meter expired while we sipped coffee at the Wimpy.

The town undoubtedly has its good points, including some BMW enthusiasts who came to shoot the breeze about bikes, but we back-tracked to Kanoneiland to look for a bed and supper. It really is an island, right in the middle of the Orange River, and was named because of a battle there between river pirates and a police contingent in 1879. The school on the island closed down some years ago and has been converted into a guesthouse called Cannon Island Tourism. With a braai sizzling and beers in hand we explored the grounds and, in the school courtyard, found the cannon that had been used to bombard the island during the battle.

::

Getting up next morning was hard work: it was freezing. Despite good leather gear the wind cut like a knife – I was thankful the bike had heated handle grips and I blessed its clever designers. Back at Upington we diverted onto the N10 and near Grootdrink we came across Agus Rots, who was making headway behind the steady tow of one-donkey and one-horse power. He was incredibly thin and wizened and his wagon badly battered.

He didn't seem too sure where he was headed – or even where he'd come from – and when we offered to send him a photo of himself he did not know where we could send it. So we asked his two grandchildren to write down their address, but they couldn't write and didn't have an address. *Karretjiemense* are the gypsies of South Africa, probably descendants of wandering Bushmen, and the road is their home. But in the far-flung emptiness of the Northern Cape it seemed a desolate existence.

At Groblershoop we turned east again and, as the road wound through some worn-looking sandstone mesas, the red dunes of the Kalahari slid across the horizon, glowing in the sinking sun. As we rolled into Griekwastad it was party time. We cut the engines on a hill overlooking the little town and the thump of inchoate rhythm and roar of voices floated up to greet us. What else can one do in Griekwastad but party? Then a throbbing, coppery moon popped up to join in the fun.

At the café in town it was quieter and we found vivacious, blonde Tania, dreaming of a boyfriend in New Zealand. We also discovered the gentle hospitality which was to endure right across the platteland. We were served coffee and offered food – which was a surprise, since most South African cafés are just grocery shops. Over a large plate of hot chips we discovered that just round the back was The Little Guest House. It was absolutely charming.

Mary Moffat, daughter of missionary extraordinaire Dr Robert Moffat, was born in Griekwastad in 1821. When the young David Livingstone set eyes on her, he was smitten and they were soon married. Poor Mary had a hard life. It's hardly surprising she turned to the bottle for solace.

There's a museum in the town dedicated to the lady and it's well worth a visit. In it, among many missionary things under the care of curator Hetta Hager, is a pulpit from which Robert Moffat preached. She says his ghost used to deliver angry sermons from the pulpit until she put a metal gate across the museum door.

We left the town in a haze of windswept dust. The road stretched out languidly across a featureless plain covered with vaalbos and sweet-thorn. Judging from the frequent road signs and black skid marks, the main inhabitants of the area are kudu devoid of road sense.

At night these large antelope with pogo-stick tendencies will try to leap over your lights and land right on top of you. I watched the verges with eagle eyes.

In Campbell, a hamlet a bit further down the road, we came upon Livingstone's Church. It had a stark new concrete floor, no pews, bird droppings everywhere and was sadly bare. A plaque outside read: 'In memory of David Livingstone, the great African explorer'. If the church is anything to go by, that memory is fading. We shrugged, kicked the bikes back into life, and hit the empty road.

::

Most people think the wind, noise and vibration are the source of the biker's exhilaration. But after 30 minutes of wind you feel no wind, after an hour of noise you hear no noise.

The vibration is slight but numbing. The wind, noise, and vibration seem to cancel each other. And in that vacuum between yourself and what's going on in the surroundings, you hang in limbo, seeing only what you want to see, feeling what you want to feel, cushioned by your thoughts and the transformation of time.

Kimberley, when it finally loomed over the table-flat horizon, was a bit of a let-down. We decided to visit the Big Hole and hunt up some lunch. The Historical Village has been carefully reconstructed, and the museums were fascinating, but the food at the so-called restaurant was appalling. In fact the whole area had a slightly sad feeling. The hole was, well, big – very big – and there's evidently an even larger one on the other side of town.

I guess we didn't really give Kimberley a chance, but it felt good to get back on the road. Around that time, it occurred to me we were becoming road junkies – as bikers often are – the roar of the exhaust and the blur of tarmac being more compelling than any desti-nation.

Motor bikes hardly touch the road and keeping them on it at speed requires intense concentration. With a car-sized engine between your legs a slight spin of the wrist can slam your body backwards as the machine accelerates to speeds seldom considered by drivers of four-wheelers. Bikes are about freedom, speed … and flying.

When Boshof appeared, though, it was time to stop. It's a cute little platteland town among the mealie fields but hardly the place you'd expect to find a first-class meal and elegant accommodation. But both were at hand.

The Gompie Café offered a fine meal and The Boshof Arms Guest House, run by Cynthia and Doug Greig, couldn't be faulted: we even got hot-water bottles. After a gargantuan breakfast the next morning we pulled the bikes onto their lawn for a wash-down. Stroking our iron steeds, we found, was a good way to get to love them.

From there it was a long leap across the feverishly busy N1 highway towards Bethlehem. Just before the town the implacable platteland began to heave uneasily and, as we crested a rise, its demise was written clear across the horizon in the jagged mountains of the

Drakensberg. The bikes gave a throaty roar of delight as the road dipped and climbed towards Clarens. This was the kind of terrain big touring bikes love. It often snows in Clarens but we were spared the pleasure. It was freezing cold, though, and it took several sherries beside the fire at Maluti Mountain Lodge to thaw out our stiff joints.

Golden Gate awaited us early the next morning. In the crisp dawn light the road snaked away from beneath our tyres like a long black tongue, leading us into the red, gaping gullet of an immense mountain serpent. The looming sandstone walls glowed with living intensity and a lammergeyer, that giant, golden vulture with flaming red eyes, wheeled above us, seeming to watch our every move. If the Great Sculptor created the platteland in a moment of boredom and the Drakensberg as an act of passion, she undoubtedly paused in Golden Gate to play.

Biking through the beetling cliffs is an extraordinary experience, but connecting up with the busy N3 between Gauteng and Durban was a nightmare. Cars, taxis and road-repair vehicles jostled for position down Van Reenen's Pass and it was a relief to turn off towards Ladysmith and Dundee.

Night was falling as we entered Dundee – it was an unscheduled stop; we'd hoped to get a little further. A café owner directed us to the Bergview Lodge, which turned out to be a sort of traveller's motel. A high steel gate and equally high wall surrounded the lodge, and at 23h00, we were told, they let out all seven dogs. Buks and Isobel Viljoen welcomed us from behind a long bar.

Perhaps because I was tired, the place seemed slightly surreal, and a post-apocalyptic film on the television a bit later didn't help to dispel the sensation. The room was comfortable, though, with the best shower of the trip. But I fell asleep feeling rather far from home.

Crossing the Buffalo River east of the town the next day was like skipping between two worlds. On the Dundee side were fenced farms with swathes of yellow grass, on the other were peasant African-hut clusters, unfenced cattle, waving children, busy pigs, sleepy donkeys and projectile sheep hurtling across the road. Driving was dangerous but interesting, and all the concentration brought on a mighty thirst. So did the heat: KwaZulu-Natal was ignoring winter. Stan's Pub in Babanango came just in time.

Stan Wintgens – who died shortly after our trip – was something of a legend and he claimed his pub to be the smallest in South Africa. He'd run the place for 25 years and it was certainly the most cluttered I'd ever seen, with 'stuff' ranging from flags and caps to women's underwear and a small wooden rabbi with an erection. The underwear, he explained, had to be taken off in the pub. The toasted sandwiches came promptly and the cider hit the counter cold and most welcome. Stan was fun. We would miss him.

From Babanango the road deteriorated as it snaked down through forest plantations. The giant logging trucks have potholed the road and the yawning traps in the tarmac surface forced us to weave around dangerously at times.

As the sun dipped low we picked our way along a confusion of roads towards Richards Bay. The dream had been to skid up to a beach beside the warm Indian Ocean, throw off our clothes and plunge into the breakers shouting: 'We've made it!' As it turned out all roads seemed to lead to the vast harbour and we couldn't find the beach. We couldn't even find the town until the next morning, and it turned out to be the sort that probably looked good on the drawing board of some town planner but had no soul.

To console ourselves we decided to spend our last night at the rather fancy Richards Hotel. The bikes looked distinctly out of place in the parking lot and highly polished luxury cars frowned rudely at our dusty camper.

Inside, the pub was more welcoming and we found the beautiful Tracy Payne in full throat at the bar where we ordered a round of celebratory whiskies. She had a great voice.

'We've biked all the way across the continent,' we called to her. 'Sing us a song.' The ballad she toasted us with had a fine blues rhythm, but it seemed a little unfair to choose Chris Rea's number 'The Road to Hell'. Perhaps she knew something about the town.

Somehow Richards Bay wasn't working for us. The next morning, as we picked our way out of town – having abandoned the beach plan – we came upon a crowd of chanting demonstrators. One held a banner saying 'We don't approve of conditions'. We didn't either, but by then we were confirmed road junkies: the destination didn't matter, the joy was in the travelling.

As we hit the N3 for the final run to Durban we cranked our throttles and watched the speedometer needles climb. It felt good to be back on the road again ... whether it led us to heaven or to hell.

Two wheels on the road to nowhere

External appearances can be misleading. Harley-Davidsons had always appeared to be glitzy, sedate, fat-seated, chrome-clad, two-wheeled conveyances for ageing men in belated pursuit of virility. As Table Mountain fell behind, I discovered a delightful truth. Harleys are wild beasts: fast, beautiful, gutsy, noisy industrial machinery with attitude – if you can conceive those contradictions.

The Road King growling down the N1 was being shoved towards warp speed by a 1450 vee-twin motor – that's bigger than my car. With a Stockman oilskin coat, new Fox leather gloves, Spitfire goggles and this monster between my legs, I felt I had all the ingredients for eternal youth. Umm, well, almost....

I was heading for Du Toit's Kloof Pass, but somehow turned off the N1 too early and instead thudded up Paarl's main street. It just went on and on.

Eventually, in a shady spot, I paused to consult a map to see where I went wrong. An old duck – her perception of motorcyclists clearly bracketing them with bad-arsed rapists or worse – tried gallantly to pretend I didn't exist.

Her diminutive dachshund, however, decided he'd have me and the bike for breakfast and did hysterical somersaults at the end of his leash, swearing insults and eventually peeing in frustration. Such is the life of a Paarl dachshund.

The object of the trip was rather obscure. I needed to get out of the city, badly, and there was a non-urgent commitment in Port Elizabeth. I could have taken a car and tootled up the Garden Route. But then there was the Harley and Route 62 through the Cape Folded Mountains into the Little Karoo. In these bergs were the outrageous Bains passes. Two wheels and Route 62 won. I'd borrowed the Harley from Ad Keukelaar of Harley Centre in Cape Town. It was his personal bike and he was being very brave. Ad had looked sympathetically at my 20-year-old Honda CX500 and suggested I'd need a few more cc's. The Road King had nearly 1000 more.

When Du Toit's Kloof was located, the Harley puttered up, disdainfully, in fifth gear. Rain had preceded me and the spectacular mountains spewed cascades of water, airbrushed to softness by whirling spray. Only pressing business could make anyone take the tunnel and miss the glory of the ramparts and these beetling cloud castles.

Solo biking is a special way to travel. The noise of the bike, the wind and the snaking road demand your total concentration. If you don't concentrate you die. Yet, in some unexplained way, a part of your mind goes into strange reverie.

Did you know that if 20th-century rates of population growth had prevailed since the invention of agriculture in 8000 BC, the earth would now be encased in a squiggling mass of human flesh, thousands of light years in diameter, expanding outwards with a radial velocity many times greater than the speed of light?

No? Oh well....

There was no squiggling mass of flesh on my bit of road. I turned off the N1 just past De Doorns and the Hex River Tunnel and from there to Montagu – for 82 kilometres – I never saw another vehicle. The only human intrusion was a sad white cross beside the road on a spectacular Burger's Pass. It read 'Kobus de Villiers' and a date. He had died three days before his 22nd birthday. I redoubled my concentration.

Riding between the farms of the Keisie Valley was a retro experience. Which century was I in? Ancient houses, old vehicles, even wizened old workers wandering down the road. Worldwide, in the last 50 years, farmland area equivalent to the size of Great Britain was paved over for roads. I hoped nobody was eyeing this bit.

The Harley and I growled into Montagu and pulled up at Montagu Country Inn, the domain of a larger-than-life enthusiast of this area, Gert Lubbe. Gert invented Route 62.

Not that the highway didn't exist before. But he couldn't figure out why anyone would want to drive from Cape Town to Port Elizabeth along the N2 – which is (protect me, Lord, from arrows or ire) boring and flat – rather than through the mountains, over a slew of passes and through 14 picturesque villages. Also he owned a hotel in Montagu, so marketing was part of the equation.

I parked the Harley beside Gert's 1956 powder-blue Cadillac De Ville. I imagined they were excited – same over-the-top style. They probably compared notes on chrome body content and the beauty of the extended trim line. Both looked so beautiful together I considered arranging a marriage, but the De Ville was too old for my Road King, so they slept in separate garages.

After dinner Gert took me for a stroll through the streets, which, at 7 o'clock, seemed to be asleep. There are many graceful old gabled Dutch houses and a scattering of Victorians. There is also a yield sign warning of cats crossing. In fact there were cats all over, most with little bells to stop them catching birds.

Beyond Montagu I was, according to the map, on Route 62 proper. The highway wound through farms and past little white shops with oversized Coca-Cola signs, then over a pass and into Tradouw Valley. Along its southern edge jagged peaks of the Langeberg range were tearing the guts out of clouds drifting up from the coast. Nut-brown cows chewed on bright green fields between orchards of peaches and apples. I stopped the thudding bike. In the shock silence could be heard the faint *doef doef* of a water pump in the river. Hadedas flew across the valley, their harsh cries echoing off the mountains, finch-song rippled in the reeds and imperative bulbuls squabbled in bluegums. The place had a Garden of Eden feel about it. The road should be lined with gawping tourists. But there was not a soul in sight.

There's a belief in Cannaland – the local name for the Little Karoo – that Montagu makes South Africa's best muscadel, Barrydale the best brandy, Ladismith the best sweet wine and Calitzdorp the best port. It's not good to drink and ride a bike so I prudently refrained from testing the claims, but Barrydale did have a fine, fruity smell as I roared through. Ronnie's Sex Shop – out past Barrydale – looked lonely in all that Karoo vastness. Inside, it proved to be a sleepy little pub adorned with lost underwear. Strange place in a strange land.

The approach to Ladismith was spectacular, dominated by the oddly split Toorkop ('bewitched peak'), a 2203-metre rampart in the Swartberg range. Calitzdorp appeared beyond the Huisrivier Pass (which tested the Harley on the corners), and after that I had Oudtshoorn in my sights.

A century ago a municipal ordinance was promulgated in these parts forbidding farmers from keeping mating pairs of ostriches where they could be seen by the public. They must have steamy courtships, but all the pairs I saw seemed to be suffering from post-coital exhaustion.

I deposited my saddlebags at the Queen's Hotel in Oudtshoorn – what a fine old establishment – then popped into the CP Nel Museum for some astounding information (small-town museums always have astounding information). Did you know that the egg of the now-extinct Madagascan elephant bird was equal to 10,000 hummingbird eggs? And that an upright ostrich egg can support 220 kilograms? No? Well, visit more country museums. (I wonder what happens at 221 kilograms?)

There was a fellow named Dykie Trook, who, in the days of the ostrich-feather boom, used to trot his horse into Oudtshoorn's shops to buy his weekly supplies, then ride up the stairs to the Imperial Hotel pub for a dram. I thought of roaring into breakfast on the Harley, but the steely eye of the concierge deterred me.

At De Rust the next day I diverted north briefly to have a look at Meiringspoort, an absolutely spectacular pass on the N12, cut through the Groot Swartberg mountains. Then I backtracked to Uniondale in the hopes of meeting the lovely hitchhiker from hell. There have been a number of reports of this beautiful young girl, who hitches a ride with motorcyclists, then simply disappears from the pillion. I must have been going the wrong way for her.

At a sleepy dorp wistfully named Avontuur (adventure), I turned back onto the R62 for the run down the Langkloof Valley to Port Elizabeth. The city was rather a shock after all that blissfully lonely countryside. I read somewhere that the number of births exceeds the number of deaths on planet Earth by 95 million. A lot of them seemed to be clustered around Port Elizabeth – or maybe I was just having an end-of-solitude downer.

In fact the city's quite pleasant, but the Harley didn't like the traffic. Business completed, I hit the road again, this time aiming down the Garden Route. The day decided to wrap itself in an unseasonable cold front. My oilskin is a wonderful coat, but at speed it becomes leaky. Fine, icy, stinging rain sliced over and under the windshield and attacked my forehead with needles.

By Storms River Bridge I'd had enough and pulled into the Tsitsikamma Restaurant, shivering and in bad repair. I was just a hair's breadth away from cursing motor bikes. It may have been my condition, but the chicken pie was the best I'd tasted. I chased it down with hot tea, then felt revived enough to look around.

After the roar of the Harley, the silence of the near-empty restaurant was a relief. But it didn't last. A busload of British tourists clattered in, making an awful racket. I watched, rather numbly, and discovered why they were so noisy. The men didn't so much converse as bid to be heard, each bidder entering the conversation louder – and before the other

speaker had finished. The two would shout for a while, then another would join the fray.

I was pondering this strange custom when a busload of Germans arrived and did the same. When they started with drinking songs I retreated to a far corner, ordered another pot of tea and watched the rain slewing down. Finally it slackened and I snitched some serviettes, wiped the Harley's saddle and took off, thankful for the quiet roar of the engine.

At The Crags it was raining again, so I huddled on the stoep of a roadside shop with a fluffed-out, grumpy-looking chicken for company. Then I splashed through Knysna and picked my way to the Belvedere Hotel to be spoiled rotten. It took a lot of courage to get out of the hot bath.

Next morning the sun dared a cloud to show its face. Damp guinea fowl voiced their approval like rusty gate hinges. At a Sedgefield filling station a bit down the road, a good-looking young girl went: 'Oh wow! What a cool bike. Can I have a ride?'

'Sure,' I offered, wondering desperately how to get rid of the rucksack tied to the pillion.

'Oh dear. Looks like there's a bag in the way,' she said. 'And anyway I don't have a helmet. But thanks for the offer. Such a nice bike....'

As my big moment wandered off, the petrol attendant gave me a stagy wink and asked: 'Can I fill her up?'

From there the road was, well, the rest of the Garden Route. Long lazy curves and straight runs along which the Harley and I hoped we wouldn't meet a speed trap.

At Albertinia I stopped at the Aloe Vera factory to buy some hand cream. 'Wouldn't you like some dog's bollocks?' the pretty, young attendant asked (she didn't say that, of course, but that's what it sounded like). 'It keeps older men fit and healthy and it's also good for prostrate problems.'

'Just the hand cream,' I said, giving her a steely look.

The bouncing bike,
the lonely Russian and the baby grand

The baby grand piano – now a bridge over a stream near Joubertina – had to do with a Russian named Richard Latti who escaped from Estonia during the First World War. His father was killed and he wanted to get as far away from the hostilities as he could. So he sailed with his mother to Cape Town, loaded all his goods, plus the piano, onto a donkey cart and kept travelling until he found a job on a farm in the Langkloof Valley near Joubertina.

He was a man of great learning, and a musician besides. He ended up owning the farm. But in a storm one year the farmhouse roof leaked and warped the piano. Latti bought another one – he couldn't bear to be without his music – but what to do with the old one? Then he hit on a good idea. The stream near his house needed to be bridged in order to get his wagon over, so he lopped off the piano's legs and dumped it in the flow.

It's still there today (though Latti is six feet under), the ivories long gone, the wood mere splinters. But the brass soundboard was still doing service as we bumped over it on the long and winding trail to Soetkraal.

We'd begun the ride at Kliphuis, an atmospheric old stone cottage on a farm along the R62 west of Joubertina. Soft boas of mist curled around the shoulders of the hills as we set out, but the sun soon consigned them to their ethereal closet.

We planned to cycle over the Langkloof Mountains along an old wagon road into a settlement named Soetkraal, deep in the lonely Palmiet River Valley, then out over another rumple of mountains – the Tsitsikamma – to the N2 at The Crags, east of Plettenberg Bay. We were being led by Kevin Evans of the Bike Shop in Plett – a demoralisingly fit rider who hardly seemed to get up a pant – and Karen McKay, whose long, whirling legs were an inspiration to any man in the party who flagged.

When I asked Kevin to rate the trail he said 'difficult'. Coming from him – a man who rides about 400 kilometres a week – that was rather daunting.

After the piano bridge and some hills – which my memory seems to have blocked out for my own protection – we topped a ridge to behold a yawning valley edged with purpling mountains. Down there, somewhere, was Soetkraal. The area was once owned by Knysna timber barons, the Thesen family, who sold it to Rand Mines. Right now it's leased to the Tsitsikamma National Park and is being heroically cleared of alien vegetation by Working for Water teams. There's nothing to mine there but there are acres of wild beauty – the Randlords should do the right thing and give it to the nation.

We hurtled down a long slope and dived into some delightful natural forest and over a bridge made from a few downed trees. Up the other side lay an old steam engine: rusted and pitched forward onto its nose. It's hard enough to get a mountain bike into those hills; heaven knows how they got that great, puffing thing there.

Soetkraal, when it appeared, was a cluster of Working for Water huts and a few ancient farm buildings. A dancing stream chuckled down the valley and the fynbos – newly liberated from a pall of black wattle and hakea – was shimmering with appreciation.

We rolled into the camp site beside the water. Kevin's dad, Leon Evans of Outeniqua Biking, had hauled tents and grub along in his Land-Rover. So all there was to do when we arrived was to leap into the brook. I'm sure it hissed when I plunked in.

Soetkraal is nestled between two ranges of mountains: Langkloof and Tsitsikamma. From the air the area looks as though the great hand of Neptune has pushed the land back from the sea, crumpling it like a giant sheet of green paper. Down its folds run rivers with names such as Bietou, Keurbooms, Palmiet and Bloukrans and – peering down at them from on high – are Thumb Peak, Witberg, Spitskop and the magnificent Formosa Peak (1675 metres).

The folds, when not invaded by Australian aliens or where Working for Water has pushed them back, are clothed in magnificent fynbos. Our way was carpeted with pelargonium, blombos, sorrel, wild dagga, erica, strawberry everlasting and buchu. As we climbed higher, sugarbush, pincushion, conebush and all manner of restios appeared. Carpenter bees zizzed round a dead, fire-blackened tree.

On the way down to Soetkraal I'd hopped off my bike when nobody else was around and listened to the sounds of the great emptiness. It was filled with the *tseep-tseep* of malachite sunbirds, the whistling of Cape sugarbirds and the insistent twitter of an orange-breasted sunbird. High above, a jackal buzzard drew a lazy curve across the valley. As I remounted it identified itself with a loud, drawn-out *weeaah-ka-ka-ka*.

The Palmiet Valley was colonised by about ten farming families in the early 1900s. They hunted, felled trees, reared cattle and cultivated wheat, sweet potatoes and oranges. But leopards and the difficulty of getting produce to markets eventually forced them out of the valley. All that's left is a few broken old houses, the rusting steam engine and interesting names such as Black Marai, Hel Hol, Maanhaar and Annie se Draai.

Next morning offered a daunting sight. The road out snaked ever upwards, over the Tsitsikamma Mountains into the clouds. Mercifully, all that condensed water overhead kept the sun at bay. To hack out there would be more than a ride: it would be a rite of passage.

The second day of any ride is never easy. This was no exception. Knees creaked, butts felt bruised, backs ached, while wide loops of road against the mountainside grinned down at us wickedly.

Kevin did what Kevin does best: he pumped up and over the mountains – never engaging low gear as far as we could make out – then rode to Plett to fetch the bike carrier and drove back with it to the foot of the mountains near The Crags. (By the time the rest of the crowd descended he'd been waiting for ages. But I'll give him this: he never crowed.)

The ride out was crazy but beautiful. There was one hill named Maanhaar which doesn't bear remembering. Each time we looked back, though, the rippling bergs and yawning valleys were ever more beautiful. Surveying the scene from the top – the sea to the south and a slew of mountains to the north – everyone expressed the same thought: 'Did I ride up there?'

Going down, despite the possibilities it promised for hotdoggery, was not pleasant. The jeep track was impossibly rutted and covered with dangerously loose stones. We bumped and banged hideously – our hands aching from clutching at the brakes – to end at the forestry station, where a grinning Kevin handed round sweet, crystallised fruit and cool juices.

That night, sitting in the comfort of Weldon Kaya Guest Lodge listening to the tinkle of a piano, I thought of Richard Latti and his baby grand. Out there, with the stream gurgling over its frame, the instrument was probably still making sweet music – a sort of never-ending fugue to the wilderness. I wondered if the old Russian could hear it.

Cycles in the forest

The huge, steaming dropping in the middle of the trail changed everything. Until then we had been enclosed in the urban busyness of unloading bikes, checking chains, adjusting saddles and engaging gears. But the pile before us suddenly made sense of the broken branches we had just passed – and jerked us out of any notions we may have had about human superiority on a narrow trail in the depths of a dark wood.

We were in the presence of a near-mythical Knysna forest elephant, the descendant of a long line of the world's southernmost herd. And, more importantly, a herd noted for its stealth and bad temper. True, the sign at the start of the Petrus se Brand cycle trail had warned of elephants. But, really, who expects those warnings to be more than tourist attractions?

The trail, which starts off along the route of an old logging railway line, was just one elephant wide and with no escape routes. If this southern beast demanded right of way we would have to ride very far and fast to oblige.

Fortunately it didn't. But as we continued, the clicks and crackles in the enclosing forest took on an added significance and upped our adrenalin count.

The old rail route was gently downhill and easy, but we were pushing hard, spurred on by a combination of early-ride exhilaration and the thought of a grumpy tusker. The damp smell of trees and forest squelch accompanied every sucking in-breath as our pumping legs demanded more oxygen. Beside us towered the sensual, silver trunks of Cape beech, goose-pimpled knobwoods and feather-barked Outeniqua yellowwoods. Then the trail dived into a part of the forest where no locomotive would dare to venture, and the click-clack of noisy gearshifts, driving the chain up the rear gear rings for more power, hushed the birdsong in the canopy above. The sudden silence overhead deepened our sense of being watched.

These are delicate, ancient, Afro-montane forests which could be said to have done a good deal of travelling themselves. They constitute a relic patch of far more extensive forests, originating in the highlands of East Africa, which hop-skipped down the eastern mountains over the millennia. Today pieces can be found in such places as the highlands of Ethiopia, the slopes of Mount Kenya, the Drakensberg and Hogsback.

These archipelagos of vegetation are the dark wombs from which spring secretive creatures: antelope, cats, apes, birds and insects. But mostly they are tireless centres of decay, recycling and gradual vegetable growth: factories which invest most of their labour in the production of huge trunks and leafy canopies. In earth's wet periods they expand, sometimes touching at their edges; in dry ones like the present they shrink back. Now roads and logging have driven these great, peaceful lungs of life to the very edge of extinction. But to be in them is still to feel the slow breath of a continent.

::

As we paused at a happy little stream seven kilometres into the ride, a green water snake zigzagged away; an omen, perhaps, of the road ahead. From here the going got tough, though not unmanageable. Gradually the wet forest with its dense fern floor gave way to a less-moist variety rising out of masses of witch-hazel.

Then the enfolding forest suddenly peeled back to deposit us in a fynbos island with views across the Keurbooms River and purple-distant Jakkalskraal Mountains. It is here that two elephants, introduced to the area in 1994, tend to wander, leaving the deepest, dark forest to a solitary old matriarch – the last of her tree-loving type. But all we found was a magnificent puddle through which to do wheelies and a table and benches in a brief shaft of sunlight to rest weary muscles.

From here a bone-jarring jeep track led us to the 14-kilometre mark: a picturesque weir over the Kleineiland River and a perfect site for lunch. It's scenes like this that make you understand what inspired the artist Thomas Baines on his travels through these parts in the 1850s. We were back in wet forest again, and stayed in it for a seemingly never-ending uphill which registered only four kilometres on the bike's computer but felt more like ten.

At 18 kilometres from the start the trail joined a road marked Stinkhoutdraai, then peeled off after a few kilometres for some of the finest downhill, single-lane forest track in the area. As the tree trunks flashed past all we could do was to pray, jumping our front wheels over tangles of wet roots which threatened to catapult us into the leafy rot or, worse, wrap us round a tree.

Finally we puffed into the appropriately named Garden of Eden, mud-covered from helmet to tread, too fired up to notice the stares of scrubbed-looking tourists with neat sandwiches and picnic flasks who'd paused alongside the N2 for a snack.

::

We were staying at the Tree-top Forest Chalet just across the road – and that turned out to be a very smart move. A shower and cold beer were near at hand and the next morning it was a perfect starting point for stage two – the Harkerville Trail.

Like Petrus se Brand, Harkerville began with its animal familiars. This time it was a troop of very large baboons which appeared on the path within ten minutes of an early-morning start. They ghosted silently into the forest: a bark would have made them seem more real. Some months previously Robbie Powell of Knysna Cycle Works had a far closer encounter. Coming round a corner of the narrow, single track at speed he was confronted by a huge male baboon. Faced with the choice of piling into the creature or slamming on his brakes he did the latter, but the front wheel dug in and he flew over his handlebars straight at the obstruction of fur and fangs. Fortunately the display contest was won by Robbie, and the baboon leapt aside and dived into the underbrush.

Our choice was the 24-kilometre red route – the green is 15 kilometres and the blue route 12 – so we first headed west and then south along Beukespad. It's a forest-enclosed single-track section which diverts briefly onto a jeep road, then plunges into the forest again down Olifantspad. The trail is well marked and excellently maintained. Logs had been stacked to ease stream crossings and, at one point, a swooping concrete strip and wooden bridge offered a river traverse which involved minimum fuss.

After a brief encounter with a belt of gum trees, we came upon a scene which makes Harkerville possibly the most spectacular mountain bike ride in the country. The forest ended abruptly and we were in waist-high fynbos overlooking plunging cliffs and the moody ocean.

From here the trail curved along the cliff edge for several kilometres. We gazed down at coves and precipices with names such as Isak se Bank, Saliepunt and Stevens Bank, listening to the roar of breakers and the *skraa* of seagulls.

At one of the trail's finest lookout points is a table with benches which demands a lunch stop. A little later, content with sandwiches, hunks of cheese, fruit and shared slabs of chocolate – and with bones still complaining from the jarring – we found it difficult to leave. If we had known what lay ahead we'd probably still be there.

From this point the trail does a last, thrilling curve, then it's low range on both gear clusters all the way up through a row of gum trees and a boring, grinding pine plantation. There's a brief downhill rush towards a stream, then it's best to numb the mind and think of something distracting and elsewhere.

Somehow the jeep track climb-out seems to be placed at precisely the point where your body demands 'enough!' But the trail keeps going, kilometre after uphill kilometre. When it finally turned back into the cool forest this salvation came too late: we'd had it. The final section to Tree-top Forest Lodge may have been beautiful, but we were beyond noticing.

Of course, one survives. Soon we were showered, a braai was crackling and hissing and cold beers were handed round. Someone once said that, had it not been for our ability to amplify the pleasure and block the memory of pain, the human race would probably not have survived. That's certainly true of Harkerville. But hindsight smooths most edges: these are some of the most exciting mountain-bike trails in South Africa. Their sheer sensuality is unforgettable, and the pain – like the shadowy creatures they harbour – soon melts away into the darkness.

In the hills of Nongqawuse

Mountain bikers dream about challenging single tracks in places few other riders have seen. Along the Wild Coast, on sleigh tracks, through crazy gorges and over historical rivers, their dreams – and a few nightmares – have a bone-jarring reality.

The Gorge had been mentioned round the Morgan Bay Hotel bar, watching an alcoholic cockatoo down dregs and steal cigarettes. Then it was just a name – no shortage of gorges along the Wild Coast. Viewed from the other end of the ride, all else would pale before that gaping green slash which the Qora River had gouged into the land – and through which we had cycled. By then 'The Gorge' would be a name about to pass into Eastern Cape cycling legend.

Chatting in the cosy pub and eyeing the odd bird, however, that challenge was several days ahead. The cockatoo lifted cans to its mouth, and even had the decency to squit off the end of the bar counter onto your feet and not next to your beer. She was named Baldy, which seemed a shame, given her magnificent yellow crest.

Early next morning we crossed the Kei River on a contraption that looked like a motorised suitcase but was, in fact, the Kei Pontoon. It had a sign which read: 'See cycads growing in the wild.' Well, why not?

Three days of single-tracking through tribal areas and forested valleys lay ahead and the weather was holding. Our destination? Qora. But where the heck was that?

The wild ride was the idea of Tony Ewels and Roger MacLachlan of African Coastal Adventures. They're both the descendants of a long line of Transkei traders and know the area and the language like, well, natives. They drummed up Candy and Brad Boonzaier, Wayne Harriss and Mike Reed, who all seemed to be connected to the Amatola Mountain Bike Club. When I saw these four adjusting their heart-rate monitors and discussing the last off-road challenge they'd trounced, I suspected they'd ride me to a wreck. I am, to be honest, a Sunday biker.

Although the Wild Coast shores are littered with other kinds of wrecks – shipwrecks – its name wasn't derived from wild seas, but from the experiences of survivors thrown up on its empty beaches far from civilisation. Ships have been trashing themselves on the rocks around there for centuries. It's estimated that along the Wild Coast there is, on average, a documented shipwreck every 1.7 kilometres.

In 1552 a Portuguese vessel, *São João*, ran aground and the survivors struggled 1600 kilometres northwards to Lourenço Marques. Few survived. A treasure ship named *Grosvenor*, laden with gold and jewels, cracked up there in 1782 and it took harrowing months for the few survivors to get to Cape Town. Their stranding coincided with the onset of the frontier wars, so all they got from local Xhosas en route was trouble. It is probably they who gave the coast its name.

The area north of the Kei River is a deeply incised landscape with precipitous valleys running seaward, the coastal strip a mosaic of forest, thicket, woodland and grassland. Because of this forbidding terrain there is no coastal road, and all access is by way of inland feeder roads. Our goal, contrary to topographic logic, was to ride the roadless coast.

Not far beyond the Kei we plunged down a precipitous track to the Gxara River, where, in 1857, the local Gcaleka people managed the opposite of the usual uprising – a sort of downslump. There was a beautiful pool into which a hissing waterfall plunged. In it, some time during the 1850s, a young girl, Nongqawuse, saw a vision which her uncle – a man of suspect character – translated into a millennial vision to rid the Gcaleka of their white oppressors. Destroy all cattle and crops, he told them, and on a certain day a blood-red sun would dawn in the west, all the ancestral warriors and their cattle would arise and the Europeans would be driven into the sea.

This coincided with the stress of a drought and cattle disease, and resonated with the Gcaleka belief that they were people who arose from the water. The valleys filled with the bellowing of stabbed cattle and the smoke of burning crops. When, on the appointed date

of 18 February 1857, the sun climbed out of the east as usual, the people knew they had been deluded. Around 30,000 died of hunger and Nongqawuse and her uncle fled. The pool still ripples strangely.

::

From the fateful Gxara Falls it was an easy ride down to the delightful, old-world Trennery's Hotel for lunch. After that we puttered by boat between towering cliffs up the Qolora River with guide Trevor Wigley, then popped in for some magical instruction from herbalist Nolokhoza. She told us she was initiated into her profession after she went mad and was healed by a certain root. She offered us some, obviously intuiting something about the mental condition of mountain bikers.

That night I fell asleep at Trennery's to the roar of breakers and their hiss as they spent their last energy up the wide beach. Early next morning we cycled to the wreck of the *Jacaranda*, a 2000-ton Greek coaster which vaulted ashore one stormy night in 1971. It came so far landwards that Captain Kokkios Paulos, his woman and 14 crewmen simply climbed down a ladder onto the rocks and strolled up the beach, leaving the good ship to its fate.

From there it was hard cycling over green hills and through river valleys all the way to Mazeppa Bay. The rivers all seemed to be named to twist a foreign tongue to insensibility: Ncizela, Kobonqaba, Nqusi, Nxaxo, Cebe, Gqunge and Nqwara. The southern Wild Coast is really unending river sculpture. They terrace, oxbow, meander or run straight as an arrow according to laws of their own making. You have a seemingly endless choice of lagoons, estuaries and deltas. The coast is green, wild and utterly beautiful. At one point Brad was probably gawking at it and missed a cue. He flew over his handlebars and used his nose as a skeg in the sand to slow down. It didn't appear to hurt him.

Mazeppa Bay Hotel is the keystone of a quaint holiday village which, but for the vehicles, could be straight out of the past century. It reeked of my childhood. There's an island with a rusty bridge I wouldn't dare cross, fishermen throwing sinkers at the sea and a beach with only occasional footprints. Purple-crested louries, masked weavers and green pigeons fussed in the dune bush, a pied kingfisher flashed past and a jackal buzzard circled overhead. A great place from which to watch a season or two.

The distance between Mazeppa Bay and Qora Mouth, our final destination, is not great as a seagull flies. But there was the small matter of The Gorge. Tony had kept warning us, at the end of each day, that the real challenge lay ahead. He wasn't kidding.

We topped a ridge next morning and stared down at the Qora River oxbowing lazily far below us, framed by surreal euphorbia trees. This was one serious slice through the hills. The single track down started thrillingly – sleigh tracks make good bike paths. But the tilt of the land got steeper and steeper until only the intrepid remained on their saddles. Some fell off.

Eventually we shouldered our bikes and picked our way down a track which is better described as a cliff. Astonishingly, Roger followed us down in his shiny new Nissan Patrol. I cannot imagine how.

Down, and still further down, until the sky was framed on all sides by hills. Riverine forest eventually swallowed us and finally the river appeared. Candy, Brad, Wayne and Mike tried to ride through. I knew my limitations and sat on the rocks taking photos of them falling into the icy water.

It needs to be recorded that, for the most part, we rode out the other side. I do not wish to remember the pain and strain of that madness, but only to recall that my four hot-shot bikers did not have to wait unduly long for me to catch up at the top. Maybe they were being kind, but it felt pretty good to gather with them at the top, peer down into The Gorge, and agree that it had been one helluva wild ride.

There was a long, winding road down to Kob Inn Hotel, another beautiful family hotel with a bar regularly sprayed by the breakers. It must be one of the few pubs from which you can catch a fish without leaving your barstool.

We showered, ordered a meal, then lifted our beers in salute to a distant, tippling cockatoo, 110 kilometres of wild track and a far-flung gorge it would take our backsides a while to forget.

INCIDENTAL JOURNEYS

Deadly dice

Missing essentials

A box of memories

Deadly dice

It was more than a matter of luck and numbers. In fact it was downright creepy. But I'm jumping ahead, so let me first explain.

Tangier Old Town is a difficult place for a Westerner. Everything seems strange: the souks crowded with men in hoods and dresses, the narrow streets of the kasbah, youngsters offering everything from ancient treasure to hashish.

My buddy and I were new to North Africa and our first reaction was paranoia. Were we going to be robbed at knifepoint? Poisoned? Kidnapped?

We rented a room for a few *diram* and went off nervously to find something to eat in the Souko Chico, the little *souk*. The eyes of swarthy men in jellabas followed us from pavement coffee shops (owned by men obviously plotting to steal our bags while we were away from our room).

On our first day a policeman approached us, introduced himself as Absalaam, and offered to sell us some high-quality *kif* (hash).

'No thanks!' I blurted, stepping back from him, amazed that he could think we could fall into such a silly trap. He looked hurt.

After a few days both of us were really uncomfortable about the sheer alienness of the city. People either treated us as potential sources of income or ignored us completely. But always there were the eyes following us from unmoving heads in coffee shops.

Quite by accident we discovered the Almohad Coffee Shop. Its entrance was a single door in a white wall with a small sign above it. I stuck my head inside and was delighted to find a square, open courtyard surrounded by cool verandas. Hooded men sat round tables drinking Turkish coffee at near-mud consistency or glasses of sweet mint tea. All conversation faded as we entered, but soon buzzed back to life. So we felt emboldened to sit down and order some tea. At almost every table the customers – all locals – were playing Ludo.

Over the next few weeks the Almohad became our local refuge. Admittedly nobody spoke to us, but after a while nobody peered at us from hooded eyes either. And the mint tea was delicious.

Then one memorable morning a large, Tuareg-looking man marched up to our table and babbled something in Arabic. Was this the moment of attack? I called the waiter over to translate.

'He has challenged you to *parchesi*.'

'What's that?' I asked, imagining a duel with matching pistols.

'That game,' he said, pointing at a Ludo board.

I must confess I'd been silently contemptuous of all these grown men playing a child's board game. Ludo, in case you don't know, consists of a board with four 'dens' in which you place four coloured counters. It takes a dice throw of six to get a counter out, after which you chase your counter round the board until you get to 'home' in the middle. The first person with all four counters home wins. As board games go, it's rather silly. The size of the man, however, didn't seem to brook refusal. I nodded, and as my buddy and I stood up so did the entire coffee shop, as if by pre-arranged signal. It was spooky.

We were ushered into seats opposite each other, and two Moroccans filled the other two opposing seats. The waiter informed us that *parchesi* was played in teams, so we had to home all our eight counters to win. It was the best of three games. The rest of the customers arranged themselves silently round the table, some even standing on chairs to get a view of the board. There was something very odd going on, but I couldn't figure out what it was.

To cut the game to a short sentence, we won the first and they won the second. In the third, decisive game, when they looked set to win, I sent one of their counters back to its den and the player couldn't seem to get a six. He eventually did, but by that time both his buddy and mine were home. I was in the home slot and he was gaining fast.

I ended up one square from home and the tension in the coffee shop was electric. Every time I rolled the dice the entire audience yelled the Arab equivalent of 'three!' It was a smart call, because a three bounced me out of home, requiring that I throw either a one or a two to win.

After I got four threes in a row my buddy and I suddenly twigged why all these grown men played Ludo. It had nothing to do with sending counters home. It was about controlling our minds and influencing the dice. This was more than a test of psychic power: we were playing for our very souls.

I threw 17 threes in succession. Each time, the room yelled 'three' and we yelled 'one' or 'two.' By then the hair on the back of my neck was stiff with fright. All logic and statistical probability flew out the top of the courtyard. Our opponent was one throw away from home. I tossed the dice and my buddy and I yelled 'one'. It spun on its corner for an indecently long time and landed with one facing up. The room erupted. We were carried shoulder high round the coffee shop, then outside into the souk. Everyone was yelling, but the only word I caught was 'parchesi'.

We spent another month in Tangier. Perfect strangers invited us to meals and kids in the streets would waggle their thumbs in the air and shout 'parchesi'. It appeared we'd trounced the local psi-wrestlers. A comment by the waiter at the Almohad Coffee Shop seemed to clear it up: 'We Arabs like people with strong minds. The dice told us you were not just tourists.'

'What would have happened if we'd lost?' I asked. His reply was a masterpiece of Arab inscrutability: 'Maybe you would then not have been able to ask that question.'

Missing essentials

It was the complaint about a missing rod on the toilet-roll holder which sparked my memory. Mrs X and her husband were holidaying on Inhaca Island in Mozambique and couldn't find the rod. The chalet also didn't have oven gloves, or a tea pot or a mixing bowl – and the fridge was held closed with an elastic strap. Imagine! So they wrote to *Getaway* about it.

Well, who can blame them? Life without a toilet-roll holder can be pretty awkward. I can remember digging a hole in the sand on the beach at Inhaca and ....

But perhaps I'd better begin elsewhere. A friend and I arrived on Inhaca when the civil war in Mozambique was too far north to be of concern. We took one look at the fancy, over-priced hotel among the palms and headed south along the beach to find a more remote spot to pitch our tent. The beach was deserted – the hotel guests were probably all looking for their mixing bowls – and our scrap of blue canvas was soon flapping in a romantic little curve of pristine African seafront.

The locals were surprised when we spoke to them. It wasn't only our bad Portuguese, it was also that in those days hotel guests pretended black locals didn't exist and never asked them things like 'where's the nearest freshwater spring?' and 'will you sell us some fish?' Which is a pity because these people had been on the island for perhaps hundreds of years and had everything there sussed out.

They showed us the spring – right near the beach – which bubbled up under a cool bush (and probably still does). They also sold us incredibly cheap dried sardines and an indescribably delicious coconut brittle they made. A little market in their village under a shaky thatched roof provided a few other peasant offerings, some of which seemed dicey and possibly illegal but nothing which killed. There were no oven gloves or toilet-roll holders but there were cashew nuts – in abundance.

I felt rather sorry for the cashew trees. A branch would give birth to a great fruit, which burst into a magnificent flower, which in turn produced a single little nut. Ever since, I have eaten cashews with restraint and great respect.

After about a month we had, in an innocent sort of way, gone completely native. Mornings were spent snorkelling over the technicolour reefs, midday we'd swap stories with the villagers or just sit under a tree and watch time pass, and by mid-afternoon we'd begin hunter-gathering for supper. On the warm star-filled evenings with the sound of the breakers and the hiss of the wave-scrubbed sand, our bellies full of fire-cooked something or other, we'd snuggle down and, well … I wasn't travelling with a business partner. There seemed little reason at all to ever leave – life was as perfect as it gets.

Which was a mistake: nature abhors human idyll. If it didn't we'd all still be Neanderthals. Without a radio, Hurricane Clara came as a complete surprise. One day the skies were Gaugin blue, the next day the clouds swatted our tent and sleeping bags right over the reef and into the bay. The sky turned late Turner and our goods just kept travelling west! We staggered back along the beach towards the hotel, contrite refugees from another age, just in time to see the screaming rim of the storm pass through the palms, steam-rolling them into the mud.

The receptionist seemed surprised that the island was otherwise inhabited – all the guests had fled a day earlier. She gave us a room for the night, having warned us that the cheaper cabins might blow away.

After a month in the palm forest, the room looked like something out of a Hollywood movie set: A bed! A bath! Toilet paper! And even a bidet! There were, I'm sure, also tea pots, a fridge with or without an elastic strap, a toilet-roll holder and possibly even oven gloves.

Somehow the bidet attracted my partner's attention. She switched it on and the stream hit the roof. So she decided to sit on it first, then open the taps; it seemed logical. But forethought should have warned that you have to get the temperature right first. What happened next should have been funny but, under the circumstances, left her badly shaken. I tried to calm her with the piped music but somehow it sounded like tin scraping. After that, everything began to jar. As the storm raged outside we sat miserably on the bed and bad-mouthed civilisation. It was illogical, of course, but there you are.

The next morning, after an uncomfortable night on a perfectly ordinary sponge mattress and a hearty breakfast which gave us indigestion, we fled. The waves were still metres high and the fishermen shook their heads, but we boarded the boat of the slightly tipsy ferryman anyway and corkscrewed hideously towards the mainland.

At a certain point my partner, who wasn't good on boats, started looking a little wild-eyed and green. Fortunately I'd anticipated this and dug into my pack, emerging with a toilet roll I'd swiped from the hotel. Out of it dropped the rod of the toilet-roll holder, which had somehow stayed inside.

The time gap is too great for me to have been the cause of Mrs X's pique, but I do understand how toilet-roll holder rods can go missing. It probably has to do with the wrong sort of people.

A box of memories

I was flabbergasted by the contents of the cardboard box in Uncle Martin's dusty Bloemfontein garage. But its eventual fate was to lead me to ponder on the very meaning of travel.

I discovered the box during one of those long, hot, holiday afternoons which induce schoolboys to dig where they're not supposed to – and I demanded an explanation. Uncle Martin, who ran the Victoria Bottle Store and was a long-suffering man, sighed and began the extraordinary tale.

My uncle's cousin Terence and his young wife, Grace, both worked on the trams in Kimberley. But the town was not spared the effects of the 1930 Depression and they were laid off work. It is not too difficult to recreate a conversation which must have ensued shortly afterwards.

'What shall we do now?' one of them would have asked.

'Let's go see the world.'

'But how? We have no money.'

'Well, we can walk....'

The thirties was an extraordinary decade. It gave birth to, among other things, outrageous architecture, innovative psychology, quirky music, expressionist art, the New Deal and fascism. However, one hardly imagines these things stirring the dust of Kimberley.

But, perhaps anticipating birth of another kind, the couple bought a pram – I could see from the pictures in the box that it was blue – loaded their few worldly possessions into it and strode north.

My brief and youthful adventure through the contents of the box did not offer me a firm bearing on their direction, but it definitely passed through the Congo and West Africa and, at some point, crossed the Straits of Gibraltar and then meandered into Spain.

The sequence of the letters and news reports in the box was pretty jumbled so just where the couple went next is still open to question. They must have passed through Europe because they gained America across the Bering Straits, which suggests they had walked clear through Russia.

Indications are that Terry and Grace worked a bit as they went and sold their stories to magazines. But they remained poor enough to still be pushing the pram by the time they got to California as a headline in a local paper attested: 'Couple Pushes Pram Round the World'. That's what had first attracted my attention when I opened the box.

At the time, I did not have enough tenacity to glean from the letters how they got to Chile (were the Straits of Magellan their goal, or the Antarctic?), but what is clear is that they'd selected Uncle Martin as the custodian of their adventures. Some four years later they were back in Europe (did they walk all the way?) and, if the pram had been replaced, it was still blue.

The decision to return home may have been a difficult one, or perhaps the couple had some plan they were working to. Anyway, the route back was through Egypt, Ethiopia and down the east coast to Durban. There, inexplicably, they took a boat to Cape Town, then set off, pram out front, for Kimberley.

Then disaster struck. About 100 miles from home Terry keeled over on the side of the road from a heart attack and died. Heaven knows what thoughts went through Grace's mind as she buried him in a farmer's field just over the fence. But she then returned to the pram and continued, stoically, to Kimberley.

Here the mystery deepens. In the box, to my memory, there were no letters from Grace in Kimberley. Did she try to put the whole episode behind her? Was she grieving for Terry to the extent that she had no further interest in the extraordinary testimony in Martin's garage? We may never know.

But the box remained in my mind for years, and I nurtured a sense that it would make one heck of a good travel book someday.

The telephone call informing me of Uncle Martin's death (my aunt had died a few years previously) caught me at a time when I was too busy to take immediate action. Two weeks later I located Martin's brother to ask him about the box (as Martin was childless the sorting of his possessions had fallen to his brother).

Yes, there had been a whole lot of junk in the garage.

'A box of papers and photographs?'

Yes, he did recall that.

'So where is it now?'

'Burned the lot, just junk,' was the reply.

I remember holding the phone, with tears rolling down my cheeks. I couldn't believe it!

That was some years ago, but before writing this tale I phoned around in an attempt to verify parts of the story. My mother vaguely remembered the couple, an uncle said he'd never heard of the trip, a cousin thought his aunt in Australia might know something....

It was clear, in the end, that all that remained of the incredible adventure was my vague memories of that hot afternoon in Bloemfontein so many years ago. And I am left with an uncomfortable question: is a journey forgotten a journey at all?

The African millennium

Ever since I met 14-year-old Marishet Dires on the bridge spanning the Blue Nile at Lake Tana in Ethiopia, he's been writing to my daughter, who is the same age as he is.

'My dearest heart friend,' he begins – and in beautiful, Amharic-laced English he chatters on about his family, his village of Bahar Dar and his hopes of being a medical doctor someday.

In Lalibela, beyond Lake Tana, I had talked to Michelle Sellassie, aged 15, about her school work. She proudly showed me an essay on the American space programme for which she'd received 80 per cent. In Kizimkazi on Zanzibar – one of the remotest places imaginable – young Salma Sulemane nDame told me she was studying hotel management in Stone Town. 'The fishing is not good anymore, and who can farm these days?' she asked. 'The future of Africa is in tourism.'

They're all normal, ambitious children who live in utterly beautiful parts of the continent: the reed-rimmed Lake Tana (the source of the Blue Nile); the mystical city of Lalibela where a king was said to have been taken up into three heavens to receive the plans for Lalibela's 13 amazing rock-hewn churches; the coral islands of the Mozambique Channel; and the Cape Peninsula – where my daughter lives – with its wonderful mountain spine and the most extraordinary plant kingdom on earth.

Africa, the continent which has nurtured them, is astounding. It has the greatest desert in the world (Sahara) and the oldest (Namib), the planet's highest free-standing mountain (Kilimanjaro), the longest river (Nile), and the world's second-largest rain forest. It also contains the greatest and most extraordinary variety of living species, the longest palaeontological record and the most complete chronicle of hominid existence.

The string of lakes up the Great Rift Valley defy description with their beauty, the mass migrations of wildebeest across the plains of Masai Maia defy comprehension and the glance of a gorilla reminds you that we are not alone on the planet.

Getaway journalists, who spend much of their time travelling Africa's roads, photographing its beauty and writing about its people and places, never fail to return from an assignment with renewed delight in the continent.

But there is a darker side which the daily news never fails to remind us. As you read this, four out of the five countries which border young Marishet's Ethiopia – and five if you include Ethiopia itself – are involved in some form of armed conflict. The war in the Congo basin seems impossible to resolve and the scale of atrocities in Sierra Leone further west is almost impossible to believe.

They're all stupid skirmishes, symptoms of the underlying problems of poverty, population pressure and political greed. And, of course, foreign arms dealers are always at hand to supply horrific fire power.

Although conflict continues to hit the headlines, it is not the continent's greatest problem. Most Africans exist by subsistence farming, and population pressure on the land is leading to denuding, soil degradation and topsoil loss. Overall, crop production is falling and is expected to be halved by 2010.

Tropical rain forests are treasure-stores of biodiversity and Africa has the second-largest in the world, totalling more than 520 million hectares and covering some 18 per cent of the land surface. However, forest destruction in Africa – from both slash-and-burn agriculture and foreign logging companies – accounts for more than 60 per cent of global defor-estation. We're losing nearly four million hectares a year. More than 75 per cent of the equatorial forests disappeared in West Africa between 1950 and 1990.

The biggest worries in Africa, which underlie all the others, however, are population and water. The United Nations has declared population the greatest threat to the world's environment. With traditional cultures and their sexual restraints crumbling, Africa has the highest population growth rate in the world (2.36 per cent). By 2150 the continent will need to support 2.8 billion people, most of them in burgeoning cities. Africa has the highest urban growth rate in the world (four per cent annually) – much of it in the Great Lakes region – and the highest number of AIDS-related deaths.

Water is a treasure without which life withers and dies. By drawing national boundaries along rivers, the colonial masters unintentionally ensured that these vital sources of water would become sites of conflict. More than 60 per cent of Africa's land area relies on shared river basins – the Congo basin, shared by 13 countries, the Niger and Nile basins by 11 each, the Zambezi and Chad basins by nine and eight countries respectively. Here poor neighbourliness often has a direct negative impact on available water and therefore on the quality of life.

It is also not good news that 40 per cent of Africa's national parks lie on international frontiers, which makes them difficult to protect.

But if Africa has its woes it is not alone. An important realisation of the 21st century is that each nation's problems are all nations' problems. Take history. In 1776 the Scottish moral philosopher and economist Adam Smith published a book, *An Inquiry into the Nature and Causes of the Wealth of Nations*. He was writing at a time when the fledgling wheels of capitalist industry in Britain were beginning to turn.

The new industrialists took comfort from Smith's words. They wanted the freedom to make profits, and Smith not only agreed they should have this freedom, he identified them as the new saviours of society – the wealth creators. He endorsed their pursuit of self-interest as being in the greatest general good.

In two hundred years industrial society, powered by that same self-interest, has penetrated the farthest, darkest corners of the land and sea and deep into space. It is irreversibly changing the great natural systems that support life on earth. Old forests topple, new deserts spread, plant and animal species are extinguished, industrial poisons penetrate even through the polar ice, billions of tons of topsoil are washed away and the human population burgeons. All this in a mere one-twenty-thousandth of the time that human life has existed on earth.

Practices based on the ideas of Smith and others like him, so alien to Africa's cooperative social systems, spawned increasing waves of slave hunters, foreign armies, miners, arms dealers, industrialists and sales reps – aided by local elites and rapacious politicians – who have worn deep tracks into its fragile soil, often leaving damaged cultures, ecological wastelands and death in their wake.

The new breed of foreigners offering aid and trade has often proved little better. A recent European-sourced investment, for example, injected US$50 million into a project based in Chad. But, because the contracts were awarded to Europeans, US$70 million was taken back out. A Malian fish project was set up but, at the end of the day, was found to have cost around US$4000 a fish. The list is long and worrying. Historian Graham Hancock has described foreign aid workers in Africa as 'lords of poverty and masters of disasters'.

For reasons such as these there are many who readily write off Africa as a basket case. But is it? The crisis in Africa undoubtedly requires radical solutions. There is no doubt that the population explosion will have to be slowed, habitat destruction curbed, drinkable water secured, food supplies ensured and corruption reduced. And if they don't bury their differences, governments will simply continue to bury their dead. Positive steps are possible, but depend on a combination of political will and sensible education – especially of women.

Given some progress on these fronts – and curbs placed on Western arms, aid, indebtedness and individual greed – there's a road the continent can take which is as obvious as it is exciting. Simply put: Africa has been attracting the wrong visitors. Those who peddle arms, aid, indebtedness and the notions of Adam Smith should be shown the door. Those who come to experience the throb and peace of the great continent should be offered a red carpet.

There is a curious hangover in this regard suffered by many of Africa's governments, South Africa included. As the rest of the world moves into a post-industrial millennium, African rulers strain their administrations and drain their coffers in pursuit of industrialisation. In doing so they are ignoring the greatest industry on earth.

Tourism presently accounts for nearly 5.5 per cent of the world's GNP and produces annual revenues of around US$2.5 trillion. Around 118 million people work in the industry, making it the world's largest employer. It's estimated that at any one time more than a million people are in the air flying somewhere.

Now consider this: a recent opinion poll in the United States shows that the number of Americans describing themselves as 'very happy' has hovered around 30 per cent since 1957, and that general satisfaction levels are falling. Reasons for this are information overload, noise pollution in cities, 9/11, war and the terrible sameness of suburban life – sheer boredom. Where the United States leads, the rest of the West (and probably the East) tends to follow.

So here's a well-informed prediction: over the next 100 years Africa – if it can get the balance right – could corner the market in two of the planet's most valuable resources: wilderness and silence. These are commodities which the richest peoples will crave and the poorest have in abundance.

Around AD 50 the Roman author of *Natural History*, Pliny the Elder, quipped that there was always something new coming out of Africa. And this is still true. But there is also something ancient: the invigorating silence of truly wild places. It's simply not a quality computers, cellphones and urban sophistication can deliver. In a sense, it's their antithesis.

Celebrated American philosopher Henry David Thoreau wrote that 'in wilderness is the preservation of the world. Not yet subdued by man, its presence refreshes him. There is the strength, the marrow, of Nature.'

Of course an ecotourist boom, if it occurred, would have its dangers: ecological and cultural pollution, the usual First World rip-offs of local operators and Western junk values. For travellers there's ropy transport, dangerous animals ... and, of course, disease.

If you are, say, an American wishing to travel to Africa, your friends will caution you about the dangers, your doctor will fill you with warnings plus every kind of prophylactic he can imagine and your insurance agent will rub her hands in glee. CNN will warn you about wars, crime and pestilence. But not to have gone to Africa is virtually not to have seen the world.

The most trustworthy guides into a new, improved millennium in Africa are, of course, our children. In this great continent I have seldom met one whose shy eyes do not soon twinkle with laughter. In their laughter there is hope, and in hope all things are possible.

Marishet Dires, writing in his small house on the shores of Lake Tana in Ethiopia, somehow expresses the dreams of all Africa when he signs off each of his letters with 'I wish you a long life on earth. May God be with you.'

I'd entrust a continent to him, any day.